"You might not put a book on e
given how everyday life is cram
families, friends, and enemies, the topic is highly important. This book will
lead you to engage with emotions in good and fruitful ways."

Ed Welch, Faculty and Counselor, Christian Counseling &
Educational Foundation

"Theologians and philosophers have often given highly oversimplified advice to people about emotions: *Subordinate them to the intellect! Welcome good emotions (joy, peace) and suppress bad (fear, anger)!* Such oversimplifications are not true to Scripture, and they hurt those who are struggling with difficult situations. Here Groves and Smith help us enormously as they untangle things, relieve confusion, and help us think through these issues in a serious way. We're enabled to see that in Scripture every emotion (whether we think of it as good or bad) has right uses and wrong ones. There is good anger and bad anger, good fear and bad fear. We're shown how to *engage* our emotions and how to act (or not act) on them. The authors have a deep understanding both of Scripture and of human experience, and they have put their insights into a strikingly well-written book, dealing with difficult questions through vivid metaphors, illustrations, and stories. Most importantly, this book is God-centered. It even contains an appendix showing us the senses in which God does and does not have feelings. I recommend this book to people who are struggling to understand their own feelings and to help others deal with theirs."

John M. Frame, Professor of Systematic Theology and Philosophy
Emeritus, Reformed Theological Seminary, Orlando

"God made us emotional beings. We love and we hate. We rejoice and we lament. We experience guilt and shame. Sometimes, maybe often, we struggle with unwanted emotions. Groves and Smith bring their considerable wisdom as counselors and students of the Bible to bear on the subject of our emotions, helping us to understand and engage our emotions and enabling us to move closer to God."

Tremper Longman III, Distinguished Scholar and Professor Emeritus,
Westmont College

"When it comes to navigating personal emotions, Groves and Smith are like river guides on a rafting trip. They understand the currents and get you where you need to go. Particularly helpful is their recognition of the link between what we feel and what we value. In my experience, that link has often been the key to unlocking complex emotions for the people I care for."

Jeremy Pierre, Chair, Department of Biblical Counseling and Family Ministry, The Southern Baptist Theological Seminary; author, *The Dynamic Heart in Daily Life*

"Steering a wise middle course between exalting and ignoring our emotions, Alasdair Groves and Winston Smith develop a biblically rich understanding of emotions as a gift from God, an essential aspect of our image bearing. But they don't stop there. With practical insight and winsome examples, they demonstrate how to evaluate and direct your emotions in ways that deepen love for God and others. If you have questions about the role of emotions in the Christian life, or if you sometimes wonder why you feel too much—or too little—of a given emotion, you will profit immensely by reading this book."

Michael R. Emlet, Faculty Member, Christian Counseling & Educational Foundation; author, *CrossTalk: Where Life and Scripture Meet* and *Descriptions and Prescriptions*

"I've been a counselor for twenty years, and I still don't get emotions. I need help to figure them out, and I'm sure you do, too. *Untangling Emotions* is now my go-to guide on emotions. It packs a lot into one book, and page after page honors Christ."

Deepak Reju, Pastor of Biblical Counseling and Family Ministry, Capitol Hill Baptist Church, Washington, DC; author, *The Pastor and Counseling* and *Preparing for Fatherhood*

"Grab this book. Dig deep. Let the Lord have your heart, for Groves and Smith are spot on: it's time we engage our emotions. Isn't it obvious that times are changing? The danger we face— Christians and pastors alike—is that we follow culture and let the love in our hearts 'grow cold' (Matt. 24:12). But this book leads us to Jesus. Its life-giving counsel—rooted in Scripture, reliant on the Lord—helps us deal with our most difficult emotions. Read this book. Embrace the process. Live it loud so we can help others—including those lost without Jesus—do the same."

Thad Rockwell Barnum, Assisting Bishop, Diocese of the Carolinas

Untangling Emotions

Untangling Emotions

J. Alasdair Groves and
Winston T. Smith

WHEATON, ILLINOIS

Library of Congress Cataloging-in-Publication Data

Names: Groves, J. Alasdair, 1982– author.
Title: Untangling emotions / J. Alasdair Groves and Winston T. Smith.
Description: Wheaton: Crossway, 2019. | Includes bibliographical references and index.
Identifiers: LCCN 2018037956 (print) | LCCN 2018053864 (ebook) | ISBN 9781433557835 (pdf) |
    ISBN 9781433557842 (mobi) | ISBN 9781433557859 (epub) | ISBN 9781433557828 (tp)
Subjects: LCSH: Emotions—Religious aspects—Christianity.
Classification: LCC BV4597.3 (ebook) | LCC BV4597.3 .G76 2019 (print) | DDC 233/.5—dc23
LC record available at https://lccn.loc.gov/2018037956

Crossway is a publishing ministry of Good News Publishers.

LB   31   30   29   28   27   26   25   24   23   22   21
15   14   13   12   11   10   9   8   7   6   5   4   3

To my mother,
who taught me to care what others felt
and to know that God cared about my heart:
You led us with faith, courage, and vulnerability
through our family's darkest hour.
—J. Alasdair Groves

———

To Kim:
Your childlike delight in the most ordinary things,
your revelry in the good and your angry tears over the bad,
your humility and faithfulness—
in these and a thousand other ways
you show me the love of Christ every day.
—Winston T. Smith

Contents

Acknowledgments

When you write a book, you realize how much of even your most creative thinking has been formed and fertilized by other people, most of whom will never realize how great their impact on you has been. How do you thank all the people who have taught you everything you know? Nevertheless, we'd like to take this opportunity to say "thank you" to a few who have especially helped us bring this project to fruition.

To Dave Dewit and the publishing team at Crossway, thank you for your patience, your input, and, most of all, your encouragement.

We are grateful as well to our colleagues at the Christian Counseling and Educational Foundation (CCEF). Your service to this institution creates a very special environment, outside of which we'd never have been able to bring these thoughts together. Thank you especially to Jayne Clark for working as our agent, to David Powlison for allowing us time to work on this book, and to the whole faculty for sharpening our thinking and affording us the chance to hone our ideas in the context of CCEF's national conference in 2016. Further specific thanks are due the School of Biblical Counseling staff team, who put up with me (Alasdair) when the book pulled me away.

To the staff and board of CCEF New England, a "thank you" as well for embracing this project and giving me (Alasdair) the freedom and support to pursue it. I needed both more than you know.

On a similar note, I (Winston) thank the congregation of St. Anne's Episcopal Church for welcoming me into your family and inviting me to take my first steps as a parish priest here. I love you all. You make me want to follow Christ more passionately each and every day.

A very special thanks to Dr. Paul Maxwell—your efforts and conversation were invaluable in shaping the material into its final form. We couldn't have done this without you! Thank you also to Andy Hanauer, Kevin and Dianna Sawyer, Susie Matter, Lauren Groves, and Alden Groves for reading parts of our manuscript in its fragile, infant, and unlovely form—you helped us to know what we meant and to say what we weren't yet saying.

Finally, our greatest "thank you" of all goes to our families. Lauren, Emily, Adara, and Alden, I (Alasdair) thank you for being excited for me and for bearing much of the stress this put on me. You are the ones I treasure most on this earth and are thus at the center of all my emotions (for better and for worse). There is no one else with whom I would rather share life's sorrows and joys. I (Winston) thank Kim, Gresham, Sydney, and Charlotte for constant love and support. Thank you for graciously accepting my shaky efforts at practicing what I talk, write, and speak about so confidently.

Introduction

How Do You Feel about How You Feel?

Emotions are strange.

They're strange in that they can make us behave in ways we don't want to. Strange in that they can flood through our bodies whether we like it or not. Strange in that they can help us see and do things we would never have done without them. Strange in that most of us don't know (or even stop to ask) *why* we are feeling what we are feeling most of the time.

And that's why we wrote this book. We want to help you understand what your emotions are (and aren't) and what you can do about it. The reality is that, while we might be slow to admit it, we're all troubled by our emotions.

Maybe your struggle is with anxiety. Maybe you're just someone who feels "stressed" a lot. Maybe you're frequently melancholy, or you live with constant low-grade frustration. Maybe life is mostly just boring. Or maybe you've never really thought about your emotions at all. It's not that hard in this day and age to flit from Netflix to email to Facebook to your job and never land anywhere in between long enough to notice that you're feeling anything.

Whatever your story, whether you know it or not, sometimes you don't like how you feel. And in that way, you're just like every other human being.

Consider a few of the different ways people experience emotions. First, take Jen. Her Tuesday morning is going just fine till a picture at the top of her Facebook feed grabs her attention. Everything about the shot of her three smiling friends, arms around the others' shoulders, proclaim that they are having a great time. The caption reads, "Girls' night out! Just what I needed!" There's just one thing missing from the picture: Jen.

Betrayal, embarrassment, surprise, anger, and a keen sense of being left out wash over her. Tears well up in her eyes, her heart begins to pound, her cheeks flush with heat. Jen can't shake the feelings and a low-grade nausea the rest of the day. *I hate this— of course no one wants to be with me*, Jen thinks. *I doubt other people feel like this. I doubt other people* are *like this.*

For others, like Angie, emotions are less like a storm and more like quicksand. Angie feels trapped in a world without ups or downs. Most often she just feels bored, empty, even numb. She has no idea why her emotions are so flat, why there's never any spark, why excitement and joy are experiences for others but not her. She always seems to be on the outside looking in. While others are enjoying a good laugh, celebrating a victory, or having a deep and satisfying conversation, she's only partially there, more a spectator than a participant. It's lonely and alienating, and she's tired of it.

Still others, like Chad, are hardly aware of their emotions at all. Sometimes he's happy, sometimes he's sad, sometimes he's angry. He can go for days without noticing what he's feeling, and he doesn't see what the fuss over emotions is all about. But his wife periodically struggles with anxiety and depression. He wishes he could help, but he doesn't know how. Chad feels more like a witness to the world of emotions than a participant and feels awkward at any significant display of emotion in others.

Finally, there's Aaron. Aaron has it pretty easy. He knows he has emotions, but they don't trouble him often. When they do, he rarely stays blue or irritated for long. He's not hiding from his deeper feelings; he just doesn't get upset all that often, and he finds that when he does, things turn out all right if he just takes a little time to let everything blow over. The sun always does seem to come out tomorrow.

So how do *you* feel about how you feel? Can you relate to any of these stories?

As we've counseled over the years, we've found that sometimes Christians are more disturbed by their emotions than non-Christians are. Christians often see negative emotions, the ones we would describe as feeling "bad," as signs of spiritual failure. Anxiety is proof that you don't trust God. Grief is failure to rest in God's good purposes for your life. Anger is just plain old selfishness. It seems that Christians are never *only* dealing with negative emotions. Instead, every dark feeling also carries with it a sense of spiritual failure, guilt, and shame about *having* that dark feeling. As a result, negative emotions are to be squashed and repented of immediately rather than explored, and should be expressed only when carefully monitored and controlled—preferably while wearing a hazmat suit.

Actually, Christians are sometimes uneasy even with positive emotions. Happiness must be scrutinized for fear of "loving the gift more than the giver," meaning God. A sense of accomplishment or satisfaction over a job well done might just be a cover for pride or taking credit for something for which we were only instruments. If you feel good for too long, it could mean you are selfish and aren't in tune with the needs of those around you.

It seems like Christians just can't seem to get it right, no matter how they feel.

The way you respond to your emotions, including how you feel about how you feel, is of vital importance to your relationship with God and others in your life. Our emotions are one of the most common and commonly misunderstood opportunities in our lives to grow in maturity and love. They have the power to deeply enrich our relationships or drive wedges into them.

Who This Book Is For

With that in mind, we hope three different kinds of people will pick up this book. First, we are writing for those whose emotions tend toward the extremes, like Jen or Angie. Both those who feel like the walking dead and those who get swept away by emotional tides have a daily need for God's comfort, help, courage, and wisdom.

Second, however, this book is for you if, like Chad, emotions baffle you. Maybe it's your own emotions you can't figure out. Maybe it's the emotional storm of a loved one. Or maybe you just can't understand why certain people in your life do the things they do, and you feel lost.

Finally, we are writing to you if you want to love and care for people whose emotions, for one reason or another, have them over a barrel. As counselors, we know how challenging it can be to care for emotionally volatile people, and we want to help you move into their lives with wisdom and practical ideas.

And what about the Aarons of the world? Do those who are happy with their emotional lives get a pass on reading this? Perhaps. But keep in mind that those with an easygoing temperament, those who are rarely forced to deal with hurt feelings, are also at risk of missing the growth and even the joy that God intends for his children in dealing with their emotions in a way that more tightly and richly connects them to him.

We believe the best way to serve you as a reader, whichever category you fall into, is to speak directly to those in the first category, those of you who struggle with your feelings and don't need anyone to tell you that emotions are challenging. Those of you in the other two groups, listen in. Don't be surprised, however, if you find that more applies to you than you had expected, and not just the "emotional people" around you. Our hope is to help all of you understand your own inner world—and that of your spouse, friend, or office-mate—better by hearing us speak to those who feel the problem of their feelings all the time and yearn to change.

Emotions Are a Gift

The Bible has a lot to teach us about emotions. It's true that Scripture warns us about the dangers of emotions, how they sometimes reflect our disordered inner world and prompt us to hasty, unwise, and destructive actions. But it also teaches us that they are an indispensable part of being human and play a crucial role in our relationships with God and others. A careful study of the Bible can help us discard faulty assumptions so we can engage our emotions rather than be ruled by or flee from them.

Here are a few of the critical truths we will be exploring together:

- *Emotions are an essential way we bear God's image.* God expresses emotions, and he designed us to express emotions too. In the Bible we see and hear God's anger, joy, sadness, and even jealousy. Of course, God does not experience emotions exactly as we do. He is spirit and doesn't have a body (an important element of our emotional lives) and is sinless, but there's no denying that he has chosen to reveal himself in the language of emotions and that our emotions are an aspect of his choice to create us to be like him.[1]
- *Jesus leads the way.* Jesus gives us a perfect picture of human emotions in action. Jesus, who is fully God, also became *fully* human. That means that Jesus knows and experiences emotions not only as God does but also as we do, as a flesh-and-blood human being. In the Gospels we witness Jesus's compassion for suffering and heartache. We see his anger as he speaks to callous religious leaders.

---

1. See the appendix, "Does God Really Feel?," for a discussion of the doctrine of God's impassibility.

We hear his groans as he grieves over unbelief and death. As we live in relationship with him, he actually begins to work in us to give us hearts increasingly like his own, hating what he hates and loving what he loves.

- *It's all about love.* Emotions have many important roles. In part, they tell us about ourselves and what's going on inside and around us. They also can provide us with the motivation and energy to take action when important things need to be done. But at the heart of all of their roles, emotions flow out of what we love, and, at the same time, they actually help us to love the right things: God and one another.

Where We're Going from Here

This book has three main sections.

Part 1 addresses the emotions of everyday life, untangling and explaining the complexity of our emotional experiences. We'll explore biblically what emotions are and what God designed them to do. As we do, you'll likely learn that some of the ways you have been taught to think about and handle your emotions need to change. We'll see how emotions involve our minds, the ways we value things, and even our bodies. We'll also learn how our emotions are an important part of how God teaches us to love one another as they help us understand and enter into each other's experiences. Perhaps most importantly, we'll learn how all of our emotions help us to turn to God and grow in our relationship with him.

Part 2 focuses on how to *engage* our emotions. This section isn't so much about how to *change* your emotions but how to respond to them and bring them wisely to God and other people. We don't want to handle emotions by being controlled by them or ignoring them; instead, we want to deal with them wisely in a way that leads to growth in our relationships with God and others.

Part 3 offers guidance on engaging the emotions that tend to trouble and confuse us the most: fear, anger, sorrow, guilt, and shame. For example, we'll explore how our anger is intended to reflect God's and actually work in our lives to protect and restore relationships. We'll discover that sadness and grief aren't always evidence of a lack of faith but, in fact, can be very important expressions of faith. We'll even find that fear isn't necessarily a bad thing but can be an expression of affection and right concern, offering us an opportunity to turn toward God.

In every chapter we'll be as practical as possible. After all, we don't just want to help you *think* differently about your emotions; we also want to help you *do* things that make a difference in your day tomorrow as you parent fussing children, enjoy coffee with friends, take out the trash, work through conflict with your spouse, sing in church, cry in the bathroom, or find a quiet moment to read. Our prayer is that as you read this book God would nurture your emotional life in the midst of both the real and troubling problems in the world around you and the real and perfect promises of God.

PART 1

UNDERSTANDING EMOTIONS

1

Sometimes It's Good to Feel Bad

Jesus wept.

That was kind of a strange thing for him to do, don't you think? We don't know how you picture Jesus, but your mental image is probably not of him wracked by sobs as tears run down his cheeks into his beard. Jesus bleeding on the cross yet forgiving his enemies? Sure. Jesus with children in his lap, smiling compassionately down? You bet. Jesus wailing loudly or shaking with silent tremors at a funeral? Not so much.

Yet that is exactly what the Bible says. Standing with Mary, the sister of his close friend Lazarus, and staring at her brother's fresh grave, Jesus is stabbed by grief and breaks down in tears (John 11:32–36). Now think about this: As God, Jesus controls the entire universe and can change anything at any time. In fact, he is going to raise Lazarus from the dead in around five minutes. Why on earth would Jesus weep when he's about to do an amazing miracle and fix the problem?

Because he's perfect. He cries at the death of his friend and is deeply moved by Mary's anguish because *that is what love does when confronted with loss.* Jesus is the only perfect human being who has ever lived, and that is why he does not refuse to share the pain of those he loves. Not even for ten minutes. Not even when he knows their sorrow is about to turn to astonished exultation.[1]

Have you ever thought about grief (or anger, or discouragement) as something that could be right and important? Even if you *could* fix the problem? It cuts against every instinct in us, doesn't it? Yet the Bible teaches over and over again that sadness, anger, dismay, and even fear have a good and right place. Most of us are deeply uncomfortable with negative feelings and assume something is wrong with us whenever we do feel sad or mad or bad. Surely, we think, if we just had more faith, a better perspective, more strength of character, we wouldn't feel this way. Or, at the very least, we'd get over it faster.

The Bible takes a radically different view. Unlike our assumption that the most faithful people will be the most carefree and emotionally upbeat, Scripture is full of aching, grieving saints who tear their clothes and sit in the ashes when their world gets upended. The basic logic in the Bible is this: if you care about others and the kingdom and mission of God in this world, you will be *and you should be* full of sorrow when you or those you love are injured, suffer loss, or die. You ought to feel angry in the presence of injustice. Your heart should beat faster when your family is in danger. As counterintuitive as it seems, awful feelings like grief can actually be exactly the right feelings to have, feelings that honor God and would be wrong *not to* feel. Christian author and thinker C. S. Lewis put this vividly when he said:

> To love at all is to be vulnerable. Love anything and your heart will be wrung and possibly broken. If you want to make sure of keeping it intact you must give it to no one, not even an animal. Wrap it carefully round with hobbies and little luxuries; avoid all entanglements. Lock it up safe in the casket or coffin of your selfishness. But in that casket, safe, dark, motionless,

---

1. We are indebted to Tim Keller for the observation that Jesus's tears flow from his perfect love.

airless, it will change. It will not be broken; it will become unbreakable, impenetrable, irredeemable.[2]

Indeed, God so loved the world that he made himself vulnerable to it, even to the point of losing his beloved Son, of sending him among us to take on our pains, weep our tears, and ultimately die the death we should have died. God loves, so God grieves. God cares for us, so he hates the sin that separates us from him. God is perfect, so he hurts when his beloved creation and precious people hurt each other and are hurt by the hurts of this hurtfully broken world.[3]

Hurt, hate, grief, and fear are terrible things to taste. What is more—as you are no doubt aware—the Bible does command joy, gratitude, contentment, peace, and the like. But that is not the whole story, and the missing pieces are vital. As strange as it seems, we have to start by understanding what is good about our negative emotions if we are ever going to handle them well when they are out of order.

Negative Emotions Are *Not* Always Bad

The basic reason we need negative, unpleasant emotions is that we live in a fallen world. God made us to respond to things as they actually are. Human beings *should* be distressed by what is distressing, horrified by violence and abuse, deeply concerned (we'd call it "anxious") about the possibility of injury to someone or something we love, angry at arrogant injustices. To *not* feel grief when someone we love dies, to not feel discouraged when we find ourselves falling into the same pattern of sin yet again, to not be upset when our children lie or hurt each other would be wrong. Even Job, the man who lost everything in a day and still worshiped

---

2. C. S. Lewis, *The Four Loves* (New York: Harcourt Brace Jovanovich, 1960), 169.
3. For those interested in a more in-depth discussion of God as "vulnerable" or "hurting," see the appendix, "Does God Really Feel?," which explains how the doctrine of "impassibility," the doctrine that God is not driven or changed by passions, is not in conflict with the way the Bible describes him as having emotions in response to the world and people he has made.

God and submitted in faith to God's control, "arose and tore his robe and shaved his head [a sign of grief] and fell on the ground" when he heard about the death of his children and the ravaging of his vast wealth (Job 1:20). You were made in the image of God himself, and that means you were made to see the world as he sees it, to respond as he responds, to hate what he hates, and to be bothered by what brings him displeasure.

That doesn't mean that godly grief or righteous anger or holy discouragement will feel pleasant! It does mean that a whole host of uncomfortable feelings can be deeply godly, right, and holy.

As if that isn't counterintuitive enough, we need to recognize the flip side of this: sometimes it's actually bad to feel good! Obviously things like cruelty (taking joy in causing pain) are wrong, but any kind of positive feeling can be warped. To be glad when someone else suffers a setback because it gets you ahead is wrong. To feel content and peaceful because you have enough heroin for another couple of days even though you're about to lose your kids is a travesty. To feel hopeful that your affair is going to stay secret is a bad thing indeed.

Seeing good in our negative emotions becomes somewhat easier when we realize God displays a whole range of negative feelings in the Bible. For example, he is described in countless places as angry or wrathful. This is hard for most of us. We feel somewhat uneasy and embarrassed by the idea that God is angry at anyone. But what kind of parents *wouldn't* be angry when someone was taking cruel pleasure in abusing their children! This wrath is exactly what the prophet Nahum, for example, recounts. He writes about God coming like a warrior against the Assyrians who had invaded Israel and were famous even in the ancient world for creative cruelty to conquered peoples. In Nahum, God comes like a SWAT team descending on a group of terrorists who have captured and tortured helpless children. If you are a helpless, abused child, God's anger on your behalf is good news. If you have suffered and been mistreated, God being upset by your pain and furious with those who have harmed you is deeply comforting.

Or think about God's grief. He is grieved in Genesis 6 when he sees the unrelenting arrogance of Adam and Eve's descendants as each passing generation becomes more violent and self-centered. Thousands of years later, in Matthew 23, Jesus mourns the sin and foolishness of his beloved Jerusalem, and he laments that these people have rejected God's loving help and correction again and again and again. And, as we observed a moment ago, Jesus weeps at the death of Lazarus his friend.

It doesn't stop with anger and grief. God is frequently "jealous" for the affection, loyalty, and worship of his people. In the garden of Gethsemane Jesus trembles and sweats blood from some combination of dread, anguish, and loneliness. The list could go on.

Here is the big idea: Our negative emotions, like God's, play a necessary role in our lives. They tell us that something is wrong. Just as happiness, joy, peace, and contentment look around and conclude that things are as they ought to be, so disgust, annoyance, discouragement, and fury are designed to identify places where this fallen world is fallen, where disorder, damage, and destruction have broken something we rightly hold precious. Evaluating the world as fractured and being moved in response are deeply *Christian* experiences.

This doesn't mean our anger or sadness always points us in the right direction—far from it, as we all know from countless personal experiences! Still, we need to understand that our darker feelings are not a curse but a gift. A dangerous gift—sometimes it feels like giving permanent markers to a toddler—but a gift nonetheless. Our emotions—all our emotions—give us the chance to share God's heart, purpose, and perspective and so to truly be his "friends," as Jesus calls the disciples at the Last Supper (John 15:15).

A day is coming when we will never again feel sorrow or anger or fear or disgust, because there will be nothing at which to be sorrowful or angry or afraid or disgusted. Until that day, however, it is only by entering into both the joys *and* the pains of God's love for his children that we can live in honest, wise relationship with the One who made us. Only those who love the Lord enough to open their hearts to the pain in his world will be able to enter into his joy as well.

Questions for Reflection

As you face your own feelings:

1. Have you ever thought of your bad feelings as having a good purpose? How does that idea strike you right now?
2. What are the most uncomfortable emotions for you to feel? Why do you think that is?
3. Would you describe yourself as a highly emotional person? As numb? As stable?

As you help others:

1. How does this chapter change the way you look at people in your life whose emotions have been a source of suffering for you?
2. Think about someone you are trying to help and love. What do this person's negative emotions say about how he or she sees the world? What specific things do this individual's emotions identify as broken, warped, or damaged?

2

What Exactly Are Emotions?

So far, we've learned that all our emotions, even the more painful and scary ones, can be good. They are part of our equipment as God's image bearers. They help us to understand and connect to the world in the same way God does and so engage it as his children, serving his purposes.

But what exactly *are* emotions?

Defining emotions is easier said than done. In fact, the debate over exactly what emotions are and what they are supposed to do is as old as philosophy itself. No joke. From the ancient Greeks like Plato and Aristotle, through the medieval and early modern periods with Thomas Aquinas and Blaise Pascal, to the modern era, there have been weighty debates about the nature and purpose of emotions.

In broad strokes, two general theories prevail.

One holds that our emotions originate in our bodies as physiological impulses or instincts to which our minds give meaning and shape. That's the general argument Plato and his followers make, and it reflects a common notion that the mind is superior to or more pure than the body. The implication is that our emotions are not to be trusted, because they come from the "animal" part of our nature, and we must use our minds, or philosophy, to master our bodies. If you are a *Star Trek* fan, you might imagine Mr. Spock making just such an argument. Though he was half-human, he learned to master his emotions (for the most part) using his Vulcan mind.

The second theory is the opposite. It argues that the way we think about and value things is reflected in our bodies. In other words, the mind is the locomotive that drives the emotions, not the body. This is often referred to as a cognitive understanding of emotions. This view doesn't assume a negative view of the body but, rather, suggests that we can manage our emotions with our minds. If you are troubled by your feelings, you need to change how you think, create a new perspective. Here you might imagine humming a few bars of "Hakuna Matata" from *The Lion King*. Exiled in the jungle with a meerkat and a warthog? Simply learn to appreciate the beauty of responsibility-free living and dining on insects. As Timon would remind us, *Hakuna matata* "means no worries for the rest of your days."

When given a choice between these two understandings, Christian thinkers usually argue that the Bible teaches a cognitive view of emotions. After all, how can the Bible apparently command us to be joyful or admonish our anger if our minds aren't in the driver's seat? That wouldn't be fair. But, as you may already suspect, things are never as neat and tidy as we would like. Sometimes it seems impossible to tease apart what is happening in the body from what is happening in the mind or to understand which comes first: what I *feel* in my body or what I *think* with my mind.

For instance, imagine you're driving home from work. It's Friday, you're looking forward to the weekend, and you're in a good mood. Suddenly, a driver swerves in front of you, forcing you to slam on the brakes. Your tires squeal as the rear of the car fishtails. Inexplicably the other driver makes a vulgar gesture at you as he speeds away.

Wait, what just happened? That doesn't make any sense! That was his fault, not yours! Fear and relief are quickly swallowed up by indignation and fury.

Minutes later you pull into your driveway and walk through the front door. The family dog faithfully greets you, jumping up on you as he invariably does, pawing at your legs, licking your fingers, and getting dog hair all over your office clothes. You immediately scream, *"Get down, you idiot! You are ruining my clothes!"* Fido slinks away and your family looks up wide-eyed and dismayed.

Your reaction even shocks you. Fido didn't do anything he doesn't do every day. He always yips and dances when you walk through the door. It usually warms your heart, even if it is a bit irritating. But today, road rage has followed you home. You know that Fido isn't the one who cut you off or insulted you, but your body and mind are engaged in a complicated emotional dance. Your body is still "angry"—your heart rate is still elevated, you feel hot, and adrenaline is still coursing through your veins. Your body is ready for a fight. (And your brain, by the way, is part of your body, so it's also shaping the way you think.) You are responding not just to the other driver but to *everything* with an angry mind-set. It really *does* irritate you when Fido jumps on you, but your body has amplified your normal irritation, which usually dissipates moments after he bounds off.

Making a tidy distinction between mind and body and assigning one as the source of emotions just doesn't fit. In any given situation one can seem more powerful than the other, and in most cases we can see how both are at work forming a kind of feedback loop. But does this really matter? Isn't this kind of a pointless philosophical debate? No, it really does matter, especially if you are looking for help with your emotions. Understanding what "causes" emotions is a critical step in learning to deal with them.

Theology of Emotions

So, does the Bible provide any clarity?

We should begin by remembering that the Bible isn't simply an encyclopedia of facts about emotions or anything else we're interested in. What the Bible "says" on any subject is part of an ongoing story about God and his people and should be understood in that context. In other words, the Bible doesn't offer a technical answer to the question What are emotions?—as if testifying before a panel of psychological researchers. We have to remember that what the Bible can teach us about emotions is there to guide us in our relationship with God and others.

Biblically, then, the question of whether emotions originate in the mind or the body isn't the central issue. Instead, the Bible places the focus on how emotions facilitate (or impede) our role as God's image bearers, helping us love him and one another (or hampering us from loving). Our emotions, in all their dimensions, body and mind, are meant to function together in a way that serves his purposes. And in that context, the Bible speaks to us as essentially unified persons, who were created with minds and bodies designed to work together seamlessly in our image-bearing tasks.

So the wisest answer to the question Do emotions originate in the mind or the body? is "probably both." Sometimes the body will seem to be the initiator or to even have the upper hand. At other times and in other situations our beliefs and interpretations will seem to be the most powerful factors. Understanding how to identify what factors are most in play and how to respond to them requires wisdom and practice.

More important to the Bible than where our emotions come from, however, is what our emotions *do*.

Communicate: Emotions Communicate Value

Perhaps one of the most important things the Bible tells us about our emotions is that they are an expression of what we value or love. Remember in the last chapter when we looked at God's good purposes even for negative emotions? Jesus's tears at Lazarus's grave and God's wrath toward those who have ravaged his people in the book of Nahum express God's love for his people and his displeasure at the ugliness of sin and the broken nature of life in this world. Both his tears and his wrath flow out of ·vhat he values or loves.

In the same way, our emotions are expressions of our own "loves" and values. Here are two examples.

First, I (Alasdair) have had a privilege many can relate to: taking a car full of small children through the drive-through window at the local bank, also known as free-lollipop land. It's quite the eye-opening lesson on how human emotions express love.

Even when my youngest was eighteen months old and couldn't yet say the word *bank*, he would begin to get excited as we pulled up to the teller's window. Some familiar looking bit of stucco wall or roof overhang apparently indicated to him that a little green or orange slice of heaven on the end of a white stick was about to magically appear over the shoulder of his car seat. Looks of excitement and anticipation sprang to the faces of my older children too. I learned that I could guarantee as much as thirty seconds of cease-fire between warring factions in the back seat by asking, "Okay, guys, who's ready for a lollipop?"

Most days the sounds of crinkling wrappers fill the car as excitement solidifies into the emotion of happiness; my children are united with the object of their love. But what happens when the middle child drops her lollipop on the floor and can't reach it? I'll tell you: weeping and gnashing of teeth. And what if the child realizes that she's dropped it because her sister was playing with the armrest and bumped her arm? Mourning morphs into anger in a flash. Then, it's up to Daddy to do something he never ever imagined himself capable of. (Ever tasted stale goldfish mixed with dirt, lint, and granola crumbs, all held together by saliva and lollipop slime? I can't recommend it.) Now reunited with her lollipop, the once-angry child feels a nameless emotion somewhere in the neighborhood of mollified but still moody.

We could keep going. The point is that even as young children, when you get what you love, you are happy. When someone else gets it, you are envious. When someone deprives you of it, you get mad. When you lose it, you grieve.

In each of these emotions, the child's love for lollipops is unchanged. The determining factor is her perspective on how that beloved lollipop is doing. While humans grow in maturity and our tastes change, the core dynamic of our emotions remains. Our feelings express our intuitive view of how well our situation is providing for and protecting what we love.

Here's a second, more serious example. I (Winston) will never forget the experience of buying my first home. I was just about to graduate from seminary. My wife, Kim, and I were embarking on a new phase of life. Everything was new and exciting, and, in addition to getting married five years earlier, this seemed like the next natural step of adulthood.

Kim approached the task with enthusiasm. She combed the newspaper for houses going on the market. She talked to friends and family about how to go about the process wisely. I was more cautious, uncertain about taking on a mortgage with an extremely tight budget, not sure I wanted to sink roots in the area.

Finally, we found what seemed like the right home. A modest fixer-upper just the right size for a couple hoping to start a small family. The morning of closing day was electric. During the walk-through we eyed every room lovingly, imagining the joy each space would contain over the coming years. In our hearts it was already ours, our beloved home. We signed the papers with excitement; our hearts were full.

Later that night we drove over to our new home, keys in hand. In the dark, things seemed different. The street was quiet. Maybe even a little spooky. The windows were dark. There was no life inside. We entered the empty house and quickly realized that, being an older home, there weren't many overhead lights. The small dining room was one of the few rooms we could illuminate. Kim sat down on the bare, hardwood floor, looked at me, and said, "I hope we've done the right thing."

"What do you mean?" I replied.

"I hope we've done the right thing," she repeated. "I mean, this is a big commitment. I hope this is the right house for us," and she started crying. I honestly don't remember how I responded, but I think I made some clumsy efforts to comfort her, though I was feeling the exact same thing.

Same day. Same house. Same hopes for the future. Two very different experiences. How do we make sense of the difference? What the house meant to us in the moment had changed. In the morning the house represented a future full of children, laughter, houseguests, gourmet coffee, and dreams come true. It was symbolic of everything good that we wanted for ourselves and future family. And that felt great. That night the house represented a future full of the unfamiliar, the unknown, financial burdens, overwhelming repairs, and risk. And that felt scary. Obviously neither the house nor our cherished desires had changed in the course of eight hours. But our perspective on and perceptions of how safe those dreams were had changed dramatically. Even down to the way we felt in our bodies. And so our emotions changed.

See the pattern? What you care about shapes what you feel. Your emotions are always expressing the things you love, value, and treasure, whether you understand them or not.

Relate: Emotions Help Us to Connect

If you had been there with Kim and me that day listening to us talk and paying attention to our emotions, you actually would have learned a lot about us. The excitement in our eyes, the frequent smiles, and the way we looked at each other and held hands as we walked through the house in the morning would have told you that we were very much in love, very much looking forward to family life together, and full of hope. That night you would have known us as young twenty-somethings, doing something new, uncertain of ourselves, still feeling the need for someone else to guide us and protect us. Our new home and our emotional responses to it actually revealed our hearts. Our emotions would have helped you to know us better. Because our emotions express our loves, hopes, dreams, fears, and so on, they actually reveal *us*, broadcasting to others—who bother to notice—who we are.

But something more might have happened as well if you were with us that day. If you had not only noticed those things but also helped us share those thoughts and feelings with you and then responded with your own emotions of care and concern, you would have *loved us* and our relationship with you would have *grown*. There is a very real sense in which sharing our emotions with each other actually strengthens our relationships.

Have you ever noticed this in your own life? Take a mental inventory of the people you feel closest to. It's likely you've had some experiences with them in which you've shared some of your deepest thoughts and feelings, or at least both experienced strong emotions.

There's a very good reason for that. Sharing in the experiences of others is fundamental to the very nature of love. Paul writes in Romans 12:9, "Let love be genuine" and then follows that with a laundry list of the many ways genuine love is expressed in relationships. He describes one of those ways in verse 15: "Rejoice with those who rejoice, weep with those who weep." In other words, one of the ways sincere love is shared is by emotionally entering into the experience of others. When they are sad, you enter into and experience their sadness. When they are happy, you enter into that happiness. Makes sense, right? If others love me, they don't just understand my experience; they are personally moved by it.

So how does Paul know this? He knows Jesus and knows that Jesus *is* love. Remember from the last chapter how Jesus's grief over Lazarus's death revealed his heart? In the same way, Jesus's willingness to enter into the grief of Lazarus's sisters was an expression of his love for them. He literally mourned with those who mourned, grieving the ugliness of sin and death and entering into the way it touched those he loved.

Motivate: Emotions Motivate Us

Emotions serve a third purpose: they give us the physical energy and motivation to do things.

If you've ever wrestled with anger, you've probably noticed that it can actually feel like a surge of energy. Your heart begins to pound, your temperature rises, and adrenalin begins to rush through your veins. Suddenly it's like you've got to actually do something about your anger. It is a call to action. That's why people so often show their anger with physical action, from shutting a drawer just a little bit harder than they needed to all the way to breaking plates and punching walls. It feels like there is energy inside demanding to be released.

Or think about the last time that you were really afraid. Your heart began to pound then too. Maybe you began to sweat. Your mouth went dry, and your palms got clammy. That was a kind of energy surge as well, but you felt more like running than fighting. If you actually did run, you probably ran faster than you would have if you weren't afraid. Your fear affected you physiologically so that if you were truly in danger, you could flee that danger.

On the other end of the spectrum, you may have noticed that a lack of emotion can mean a lack of energy or will to act. If you've ever suffered from depression, you know how debilitating it can be, in the sense that you not only are in emotional pain or feel flat but also find it difficult to do anything, perhaps even get out of the bed in the morning.

This motivational aspect of our emotions is God's way of helping us put our values into action. Through the energy anger provides, whether to intervene in a perceived wrong or to flee a dangerous situation, our emotions are constantly spurring us to further God's purposes in our lives.

Elevate: Emotions Turn Us toward God

The previous three categories all emphasize how our emotions help us to interact and connect with our core values, the world around us, and even our physical bodies. But our emotions perform another role that underlies and shapes the other three: our emotions reveal our connection to God. Or put another way, *our emotions are an expression of worship.*

That may strike you as odd. For many of us, the word *worship* is essentially synonymous with singing songs on a Sunday morning, and the musical portion of the service is called worship in contrast to the sermon or announcements or communion. In other words, for many, worship is limited to emotion-filled musical moments and is something that helps us feel a particular way about God. But worship is bigger than any particular experience or subset of emotions.

In fact, Scripture teaches that whether we think of ourselves as religious or not, we are worshiping at all times. Jesus gets at this in his summary of the law. When asked what the greatest commandment of the law is, he responds, "You shall love the Lord your God with all your heart and with all your soul and with all your mind. This is the great and first commandment. And a second is like it: You shall love your neighbor as yourself. On these two commandments depend all the Law and the Prophets" (Matt. 22:36–40).

Jesus is addressing the way we tend to ignore the commandments that we don't like. In particular, the religious leaders he is debating love the ceremonial ritual of worship and the honor they receive as leaders, but they don't love people; they exploit them.[1] He is telling us that in our relationships, whether with God or with our neighbor, God's commandment to love applies at all times.

So, essentially, the first great commandment describes our duty to worship. We should love God with all that we are, every element of our lives—heart, soul, mind, and strength. The second

---

1. See Matt. 23:1–36.

great commandment is like it in that it is an extension or application of the first. Our worship or love of God must be reflected in the way we treat others. So we can't segment our lives into pieces and call one of those pieces worship. That doesn't mean that we shouldn't love people or things other than God. But our love for God should shape all our other loves or commitments. If we are loving something else more than God, letting it call the shots and guide our lives, it is functioning like God to us. But whether our greatest love is God or something else, it is essentially what is driving us and so the true object of our worship.

Here, then, is what this means: every emotion you ever feel reflects your loves, or what you worship. This is easy to see in terms of joy, thanks, and awe. But it's equally true of sorrow, guilt, and distress! Where godly joy, for example, flows from a heart that treasures what God treasures and sees God's purposes advancing, godly distress comes from a heart that treasures what God treasures and sees his will being violated. Godly distress is the cry of a heart that honors God's desires as good ones, honors God's will as right, and is so personally committed to seeing God's will being done on earth as it is in heaven that it causes anguish of spirit to see the opposite.

Godly joy and godly distress *both* reflect godly worship.

All unpleasant emotions can work this way. Righteous guilt honors the goodness of God's law. Righteous grief has tasted and seen that God is good, and that the loss of his good gifts is painful. Because worship of God places ultimate value on him, all godly painful emotions actually serve to communicate that value, more firmly establish us in relationship with him, and motivate us to obey.

Ultimately every emotion reflects our worship, that is, the loves or commitments of our hearts. But sometimes our worship is off. We love the wrong thing, or maybe we love the right things in the wrong way or too much. Not everything we feel flows from a value for what God loves, but every point on our whole spectrum of emotions was designed to send us sprinting to our Father with words like "thank you," "help me," "you're amazing," or "oh no!" No feeling is beyond redemption. Every feeling that turns toward God actually becomes part of our worship.

But don't unbuckle your seat belt just yet—the ride isn't over! In fact, things get even more exciting in the next chapter as we explore the ways our emotions interact *with each other.*

Questions for Reflection

As you face your own feelings:

1.   What is the most recent emotion you remember feeling? What did it communicate about what you value? What action(s) did it push you toward? How did it, or could it, impact your relationships with other people? In what way did it turn you toward (or away from) God?

As you help others:

1.   Do you believe that "negative" emotions can lead people toward right actions? Can you think of an example you've seen?
2.   Think about the last time you experienced someone else feeling strong emotions. What were those emotions communicating? Was that easy to see, or hard?

3

Emotions Don't Come in Single File

Even if you followed every bit of the previous chapter, you still can probably come up with quite a few situations where it's difficult to see exactly what your emotions were trying to communicate, or why you felt so upset about something, or why you went into a downward spiral in response to something that happened many times before without causing such a problem.

While we sometimes struggle to understand our feelings because we are blind to what we are really loving, more often the confusion has a different source: our emotions never come in single file! Life isn't that simple. The vast majority of the time, human beings are awash with different, even conflicting emotions. Sure, sometimes you might make some clear, one-to-one connections between an experience and the emotion you feel as a result. For example, you might recognize that you are angry because someone ignored or insulted your child. Or you might realize your sudden feeling of sadness came from the smell of mothballs, which reminded you of your beloved grandparents' house in the country and the fact you won't ever be there again, now that they're gone.

Most often, however, you aren't responding to just one thing (and even when you are, there's stuff going on in the background). That makes it really hard to know what you are feeling. Even in counseling, where people have both time and guided encouragement to slow down and process their feelings, the most frequent thing they say about them is "I'm not quite sure what I'm feeling right now."

Confusion about what you are feeling and why you are feeling it is very normal.

The reason is simple: *you love lots of things.* If what you love and care about shapes what you feel, then the fact that you love *many* things means you are always going to be simultaneously responding to different pieces of the world around you differently. While you will find that the cares connected to whatever you've focused your attention on have the biggest impact on your emotions, you'll also find that other cares and other situations are always present in the background to some degree.

That's why your response to your toddler spilling her cup on the floor will be different on different days. You're being affected by a thousand factors just from this morning: how you slept last night, what terms you and your husband were on when he left for work, how you felt about pictures of your friends' families on Facebook, what you had for breakfast, whether you have a packed schedule or a relaxed day, and so on. You'll either clench your teeth or smile and shake your head based not just on how you feel toward your child's spill but on your feelings about everything else too.

Don't Run from Complexity

Most people respond to this complexity by oversimplifying in one of two basic ways. On one end of the spectrum are those who largely ignore emotions and "just move on" or "get over it." They tend to deal with life by taking action, focusing on what they can *do*, not what they feel. Sometimes this is because, after enough years, they aren't even aware they have emotions. At other times people on this end of the spectrum know there are emotions float-ing around inside somewhere, but chasing after them feels like a waste of time. Life feels much simpler when you steer clear of the uncharted and uncomfortable sea of your emotions.

On the other end of the spectrum are those who oversimplify in the opposite direction. Instead of ignoring emotions in favor of actions, they focus intensely on their emotions—which tend to dominate everything else in their lives—and deal with them by hunting down a bad guy to blame. Sometimes these people condemn themselves as the bad guy. Because I have a negative emotional reaction, the thinking goes, there must be something wrong with me. At other times they condemn everyone and ev-erything else around them (or seesaw from one to the other in the space of a moment). Either way, instead of sifting through the many different aspects of the situation that their negative reaction is based on—a bad night's sleep, a child in trouble at school, an inconsiderate coworker, the strain of packing and moving, and so on are real trials that *rightly* upset you to some degree—this end of the spectrum takes an all-or-nothing approach. If it's bad at all, it's all bad. If I'm wrong at all, I'm all wrong. If I feel bothered by something you've done, you're a dangerous enemy. Because this oversimplification almost always misses aspects of what is going on, even though those who lean this way may be aware of their emotions, they're often confused about why they feel upset.

To help you see the importance of *not* oversimplifying, con-sider Ellen. Ellen was feeling upset that although her daughter was in the home stretch of her senior year in high school, Ellen couldn't seem to feel any joy or excitement for her daughter. As her daughter picked out a prom dress, signed yearbooks, went on a senior class trip, and counted down the days to graduation, Ellen condemned herself over and over again with a self-imposed judgment: "you are a terrible and cold-hearted mother."

The problem with her self-prosecuted case was that it contained a gaping hole. The reason she couldn't enter into her daughter's joy

was that her other daughter was facing major and extremely painful surgery to correct the problems of an earlier surgery that failed.
Without realizing it, Ellen actually *was* feeling happy and
excited for her daughter. But her joy for her daughter was so
drowned out by concern and fear for her other daughter, she was
barely aware of that joy. She deeply loves both girls, but the grav-
ity of her sick daughter's condition was so severe that her attention
was understandably absorbed there. So Ellen felt constant guilt
and sadness that she was failing her happy child.

Ellen, you see, was really uncomfortable with the idea that
she could have multiple emotions at the same time. Knowing,
both from the Bible and from her own gut instincts, that she was
supposed to "rejoice with those who rejoice," she interpreted
the mix of gladness and sadness as a failure to rejoice and thus
ultimately a failure to love her graduate. It seemed simple and
condemning: she *ought* to have felt excited for her older daughter, she *wanted* to be excited for her, but she *wasn't* feeling an
easy, sustained excitement; she was allowing her "negativity" to
dominate her, and *therefore* she was a bad mother. Case closed.
The result was a great tragedy: Ellen's emotions were now mixing in a steady stream of guilt that further confused her and was
poisoning both her godly joy for her one daughter and her godly
sorrow for the other!

Jesus Had Mixed Emotions

Jesus himself was no stranger to mixed emotions. This should
come as no surprise: because Jesus loved his Father and his fellow
human beings perfectly, we should expect him to have had more
intensely mixed emotions than anyone else. He ought to have
been angrier than anyone else in the presence of evil, and more
overjoyed than anyone else to witness the fruit of the Spirit. And
that is exactly what we find.

Think yet again about Jesus's grief at the tomb of Lazarus.
Jesus loved Mary, so he grieved her loss. But he also hated sin

and death, so he felt deep anger. Further, he had already told the disciples that this miracle was going to be a great blessing to their faith, and, because he loved them too, he also felt some level of excitement in the background for the good this would do them.

Or take Matthew 23, where Jesus lays into the Pharisees and teachers of the law for their hypocrisy and hard hearts with his most extended, sledgehammer-like rebuke. But then, after thirty-some verses of intense critique, Jesus gives voice to one of the most poignant laments in all of Scripture, his heart overflowing with compassion for the very people he has just chastised: "O Jerusalem, Jerusalem, the city that kills the prophets and stones those who are sent to it! How often would I have gathered your children together as a hen gathers her brood under her wings, and you were not willing!" (Matt. 23:37). His love for the people of God leads him to be furious with the corruption of their leaders. That same love simultaneously leads him to deeply grieve that those leaders are blind to what could heal them. This is full-throttle anger, heart-wrenching compassion, and profound grief pouring together from Jesus's heart, for the very same people!

We could give many more examples. The bottom line is this: mixed emotions are the *right* response to a mixed world. Life in this world means the delightful glories of God's handiwork always get the muck of sin and suffering spattered on them. We have no godly choice but to both mourn and rejoice.

By beating herself up for feeling anything less than carefree happiness with her daughter, my friend Ellen was fighting against the reality that joy for what is good and grief or concern for what is bad can and should coexist in the same heart. Seeing all this, of course, took her some time. Initially Ellen wrapped up all these feelings in one word, saying she felt "confused." It was a good summary. What helped her was the realization that she didn't have to feel only one thing, that she was actually right to mourn *and* rejoice, and that her rejoicing was not wrong for being tinged with grief. Grasping this, she began to seek opportunities to share her one daughter's excitement where she could without trying to banish grief and concern for the other. It was difficult, of course, but it was a shift she desperately needed to make. She let go of the impossible and unhelpful goal of not being affected by her younger daughter's pain, and held on instead to the challenging but worthy goal of loving and living with two cherished children at the same time.

For some of you, the idea that we feel all sorts of things at the same time will seem strange or even wrong. Others of you live in a constantly rolling kaleidoscope of emotion, and nothing could be more obvious to you than the fact that you feel many things at once. Even then, however, the mixing of emotions feels like a bad thing, and you mourn your inability to feel what you are sure "normal" people feel (i.e., one thing at a time, nothing too overwhelming).

The counterintuitive reality is that joy and sorrow really can deeply mingle. You are allowed to feel deep grief and deep joy at the same time. Christians are called to grieve with hope (1 Thess. 4:13). Compassion and anger, joy and sorrow, various kinds of grief and a hundred more emotions need to be able to flow together, as they often did for Jesus.

Emotions Mix Like Paint Colors

Think of it this way: human emotions mix much like streams of paint flowing into a bucket. Have you ever been to a Home Depot or a paint store and requested a custom color? When you ask for Evergreen or Colonial Blue, the paint tech takes your bucket of white paint, puts it under a machine, and punches in the code for your desired hue. Then the computer obligingly tells several tint canisters to pour specific amounts of dense color into your paint bucket. When the computer hits the precise amount of each colorant, it shuts off, and, voilà, you have your gallon of custom paint. A touch more black or a drop of crimson withheld, and you'd have some other color one shade away.

Your emotional state at any moment is like that paint bucket with streams pouring into it from your heart. Your heart is pouring out a stream of emotion (sometimes as just a trickle, sometimes as a torrent) for every care you have. The machine at the paint store has only a few nozzles, of course, but your heart has thousands of different pipes carrying color into the mix of what you feel.

Thus, your emotions at any moment are a mix of your responses to everything around you! You're influenced by whether it is sunny or cloudy, whether your job is going well or poorly, whether your coworkers are easy to get along with or standoffish, whether your kids slept well last night or were up a lot, whether you had a refreshing devotional time that softened your heart toward the Lord or read a passage that confused and upset you (or haven't opened a Bible since you were fourteen at summer camp). Your emotions are responding to the tone of voice your mom used on the phone last week when she asked about that ongoing sensitive situation, to your own thoughts about where you'll be in ten years, to the traffic, to the season, to the likelihood of having time to play your new board game, to how much time you'll have to work in the woodshop, to whether that new dress fits as well as you thought it might, to how much you owe in taxes (and how long you have till April 15th!), to whether God exists or not and what that has to do with you, to whether your sandwich at lunch is too bland or too spicy, and on and on and on.

The list of things our hearts are responding to is literally endless. Obviously these issues are not all the same size, and the amount of color pouring out of your heart and into your bucket will vary enormously based on how important it is to you that your sandwich taste good, or that your mother think well of you, or that you have a relationship with the God of the universe. The point, for now, is that each of these concerns is a little jet of color dripping, or gushing, into your bucket of emotional paint.

Now here's the thing: However many streams are pouring in, it's all getting swirled together. Unlike the paint store, there is no shutoff to this process; your heart is never going to stop pouring emotion into your life! Specific pipes might shut off for a minute or a decade, but your heart will always be pouring forth many streams, because you are always going to care about what happens to you and around you (like we said in the last chapter). At the end of the day, the way you answer the question How are you feeling? is going to be your attempt to capture all those swirling, intermingling colors in one big summary. And, as anyone who has ever stared at a paint chip display and said, "Is that orange? Or brown? Or, I guess, beige? What do you think?" can tell you, trying to fit a name onto a blend is no easy task, even when that blend isn't constantly changing.

Let's look at an example of how this could play out in real life. Imagine three different people doing some mundane task, say, standing at the sink doing dishes—not the kind of thing most of us would think of as an emotional experience. Watch how even something as normal as a daily household chore can be a melting pot for all kinds of emotions.

First, picture a young woman whose roommate just moved out a few weeks ago. She might describe herself as feeling lonely. Clinking dishes and running water sound louder in an apartment that somehow feels emptier now. Having fewer dishes in the sink reminds her that she is by herself. Yet, though she admits it only to herself, she is also relieved to be done with the annoyance of a messy roommate who often left her dishes in the sink. Fewer dishes are not just a reminder of being alone but also a symbol of newfound freedom, privacy, and relief from hassle. *But who feels glad about getting rid of a perfectly sweet roommate?* she asks herself, and the guilt faucet opens too. Loneliness, relieved excitement, and guilt—not a simple sauce to simmer.

The second dish scrubber is a married man, and his emotional bucket is filling with fury faster than the sink is filling with suds. You wouldn't want to be the pot he is attacking with that Brillo pad. He's angrily scrubbing because he and his wife just had a fight, and he's playing the tape over and over in his head, unaware that he is tense in every muscle and scouring cups hard enough to break them. *Yet again* she made something utterly trivial into a huge deal, he thinks. *Yet again* she wouldn't listen to his side. It's not that this fight was so awful; it's that it happened *yet again* and that, even though she started it, he'll now have to deal with her in a funk for who knows how long *yet again*. But he's scared too. Their anniversary is Saturday, and he has put a decent amount of money and time into planning a weekend away. If they leave like this, it's going to be miserable, and he's been really hoping this weekend would help their marriage and ease the tension that always seems to be there these days. This man's dishes (it's the first time he's done them in a while) are part punching bag, part peace offering, and part outlet for nervous energy.

Finally, picture a young mother of three at the sink, a burp cloth tucked into her back pocket and a fussing toddler clinging to her leg. If you asked her, "What are you feeling right now?" and she'd had enough coffee that morning to form a coherent sentence, she might say: "I don't have *time* to feel anything—could you pass me the dish towel please? It's over there where the orange juice spilled." Her dishes dance through the sink in a blur, but she is feeling (though not consciously thinking) how futile it is to clean anything—it all just gets dirty again. This woman's dishes are an emblem of the wearisome, monotonous stress of life. At the same time, they represent the fulfillment of her life's dream to be a mom. Her life, like her harried attempt to cram the oatmeal-caked bowls and the sippy cups into the dishwasher, is a constant swirl of satisfaction at tangible tasks accomplished, frustration at messes and fusses, and throwing up her hands at a to-do list that never ends or gets shorter. She simultaneously feels weighed down (a feeling her sleep-deprived body is only too happy to amplify), genuine happiness to be with her kids and making a home for her family, and disappointment at the way motherhood never quite plays out like she had dreamed.

It really is complicated, isn't it? Even with all the things going on in these three stories, we're only scratching the surface. We've only identified a few major and especially relevant cares each person is responding to. We haven't told you anything about their childhood, their faith, what country they live in, and so on. How they respond to those factors and a thousand more all go into determining the exact tint of their emotions.

Every so often, of course, one aspect of your world seizes center stage, and a single emotion dominates. Weddings, funerals, special birthday presents, and losing your purse all have a way of grabbing your full attention. Yet even these sudden surges of one color overwhelm and define the mix for only a moment; they don't pour into an empty bucket. Each of us contains an emotional pool that's had paint sloshing in since the day we were born!

Where to from Here?

In the next chapter we'll look at how our feelings in these God-created physical bodies can further tinge the mix of colors in our bucket. For now, however, we simply need to understand two things clearly.

First, we want to understand as much as we can about anything in our emotional buckets. The more we know about what's going on in the swish and swirl of our feelings, the better we'll be able to understand what is going on in our hearts and our loves. Every little bit helps. Second, however, we need to remember that we will never exhaustively understand all the streams from our hearts into our emotions, and we don't need to! Instead, all we need to do is bring whatever we do manage to understand to God and entrust him with all the hidden corners of our hearts, loves, and feelings that we can't see into but he knows perfectly. Part 2 of this book will focus on how to do this in depth, and we are getting there! We just have a few last pieces of the foundation to lay.

Questions for Reflection

As you face your own feelings:

1. What streams of emotion pouring into your emotional bucket today can you name?

2. Does the idea of feeling many things at once overwhelm you? Seem untrue? Feel liberating? Why?

3. If you can't identify any emotions in yourself, ask your spouse, a church leader who knows you, or one or two close friends what emotions they've seen in you, or what they guess you've been feeling. Does their answer make sense to you? Why, or why not?

As you help others:

1. How would you explain to someone why it is not just inevitable but actually good that he or she feels mixed emotions?

2. What are the dangers of ignoring the mixed nature of someone's emotions? What are the dangers of trying endlessly to identify every stream pouring into the bucket?

4

Emotions Happen in Your Body

The complexity of emotions means that literally countless things—we've mentioned the weather, the tone of your spouse's voice, and tax deadlines, just to name three—impact them. However, two particular influences on our emotions (other than God himself) especially stand out for the constancy of their influence on our lives from the day we are born till the day we die: our bodies and our communities. We'll take the next two chapters to zoom in on these two aspects of human existence and how each interacts with our emotions. This chapter will focus on the body.

Bodies Matter

Your emotions don't happen in the abstract; they happen *in your body*. Responding with emotion to something literally causes a physical reaction in your skin, your brain, and your blood. Have you ever stopped to reflect on just how odd, how nearly magical this is? Someone can say words into a phone a thousand miles away and make the hair on the back of your neck stand up. The simple sight of a photograph can reach into your chest and make your heart pound. That we can change the flow of another person's blood and brain chemistry by using mere syllables is a testimony to how profoundly God has made us creatures of meaning, beings whose lives and loves matter. Our bodies are the messengers of our souls, and they cry aloud over and over again that we care deeply about the purpose, outcome, and experiences of our lives.

In this sense, your body acts as a billboard displaying your emotions to you and the world (whether you want it to or not). Your body clearly worries that if it doesn't capture your attention, you might not listen to your heart's messages. Your emotions are always going physical, hanging out flashing signs in the form of frowns, grins, tears, sweat, racing heartbeats, surging adrenaline, spiking body temperatures, clenched jaws, tense shoulders, and dilating pupils, announcing that something has happened to something you care about. It is no accident that so many clichés about emotions are descriptions of something happening to your body; we all know what it means when the blood drains from someone's face, someone has a sinking feeling in the pit of the stomach, or someone's body feels light and energized enough to walk on air.

The influence between emotions and body, however, goes both ways: not only can our emotions call forth physical changes in our bodies, but changes in our physical bodies can have an impact on our emotions. In fact, *anything* that happens to us physically is likely to have some effect on our emotions. For example, have you ever been walking to the fridge and had your pleasant anticipation of a good snack turn into a minor rage at something like stubbing your toe on the backpack your roommate left in your path? It's amazing how a simple pain in just one digit of just one of your feet can drain joy and flood your mind with anger at your roommate's lack of organization and consideration.

Bodies Are Good

It's easiest to think of *negative* ways your body can affect your emotions, but this does not mean your body's impact is always a problem! On the contrary, as common sense suggests, regular exercise, sufficient sleep, being warm (or cool) enough, having a full (but not stuffed) belly, and a hundred other physiological experiences make it easier for our emotions to line up with God's. While our pains can draw us to God as well, which we'll talk more about in part 2, it's worth reminding ourselves of the obvious: healthy bodies tend to amplify healthy worship. It is all too easy to forget that Christians have every reason to be thankful for God's choice to clothe our souls in flesh, even when it comes to our emotions.

This is important because Christians have tended to have an uneasy relationship with bodies. Most Christians are suspicious of desires and feelings that come primarily from our bodies. And, let's be honest, this is understandable. We've all been sluggish getting out of bed, had an extra cookie, failed to check angry words pouring out of our mouths, or found ourselves cultivating some secret and compelling sexual temptation. Our bodily desires often get us in trouble.

Thus, while we are right to be suspicious of the way our bodies tug us away from God in the wake of the fall of the human race into sin, it is equally important to remind ourselves that our bodies are good! Having a human body was God's idea, and he pronounced it "good," like the rest of created existence. Having emotions that motivate our behavior is not a product of being sinners. You were *made* to desire and to emote. The problem is not that your body has emotions. The problem is that your body, like your mind, soul, and strength, has been affected by sin and has a skewing effect on your emotions.

In short, while we are going to focus on the problems our bodies cause for our feelings, we want you to keep firmly in mind that our bodies are not an embarrassment, nor are they fundamentally a problem. In God's kindness, he has wired our emotions to constantly capture our attention (quite dramatically sometimes) and keep it where it needs to be. Without bodies full of emotion, we would put vastly less effort into relationships (sadness, anger, happiness, laughter, etc. all drive us toward loving others well), seeking God (love for God and neighbor both demand emotion by definition), and worshiping him (gratitude, awe, delight, lament are all emotions that drive our praise).

Bodies Go Wrong

Our starting point, then, is that bodies are good, our physical experience of emotions is good, and even our ability to feel negative emotions in our bodies is a good part of God's design of us as his image bearers. That said, we are all only too aware that our bodies' contributions to emotions do *not* always lead to good. So let's take a look at the three basic ways our physiology can impair our emotions.

Too Fast or Too Slow

Emotions are instinctive; we hardly ever consciously choose what to feel (and are rarely successful when we try). This is another good and right aspect of God's design! You were made to live out of love. The more you love, the more you'll respond immediately when something affects what you love. Thus, when fear catapults you quicker than thought toward your child who is stepping into the street, you are experiencing God's blessing of *instinctive* emotions. (More on the instinctive nature of emotions in chap. 6.)

Sometimes, however, they come too fast. A trivial trigger (the smell of coffee brewing, cars shifting lanes too quickly, a face or voice similar to that of an abuser, etc.) can evoke an intense response in you before you even know what the trigger was. Such lightning-quick reflexes most often develop over time in response to severe or chronic suffering. Our bodies, given practice, learn to activate a red alert at the slightest provocation. And well they should! We ought to be horrified by what is horrifying, fight or flee from what is dangerous, and exult in what is glorious.

I (Alasdair) remember one particular counseling situation where someone was sending me frequent accusatory emails I needed to respond to. Over the course of a mere week I got to the point where my heart would race and I would almost physically jump every time *any* new email popped up in my inbox. My body had adjusted to a situation where what I valued (being at peace in relationships, not having people angry at me, etc.) was threatened, and my heart rate and muscle tensing began to burst into action before my brain could even process the name of the email sender on my screen.

On the other hand, sometimes emotions come too slowly or not at all. Just as in severe physical trauma your body can go into shock, dampening pain, decreasing blood flow, and turning off non-vital functions, so your emotions sometimes essentially shut down in the face of perceived loss or threat. This is what is happening when a woman seems surprisingly fine in the immediate aftermath of her husband's death as she cares for her children, organizes funeral details, and shows up for work, but then completely melts down nine months later. This kind of delayed reaction can happen on a smaller scale too. I (Alasdair) remember going to lunch with a girl I had a crush on, only to have her drop a bombshell on me by telling me she had just started dating someone else the night before. For the rest of lunch I managed to keep up a conversation, but I had emotionally flatlined and I couldn't have told you one thing we talked about to save my life. It wasn't till after I dropped her off an hour later that grief, frustration, embarrassment, and the like started to flood in.

In short, God made us to respond to the world around us *in the moment,* our hearts and bodies responding to our construal of how our situation is affecting the things we most love.[1] When our bodies rush or delay that reaction, we begin to drift out of rhythm with reality, and our emotions start to pull us away from worshipful, trusting obedience rather than toward it.

---

1. We have appreciated Robert C. Roberts's language of "construal" for how our perspective shapes our emotion. Roberts defines emotions as "concern-based construals," meaning that our concerns (what we are calling "loves") turn into emotions based on how we *construe* our situation. For readers interested in a more philosophical and technical examination of the intersection of emotion and Christian faith, we recommend Roberts, *Spiritual Emotions: A Psychology of Christian Virtues* (Grand Rapids, MI: Eerdmans, 2007), Kindle.

Too Long or Too Short

Just as the speed with which our emotions come (or don't come) can cause problems, so can the duration of their stay. Because God gave us emotions to energize our obedience, it is a problem when that energy abandons us before we've fully followed through, or keeps pumping and fueling action after the need for that particular obedience has passed. We all experience both.

Emotions peter out too quickly all the time. Think, for example, about the last time you got inspired to clean up your office or your fridge, call an old friend, or donate to that hurricane relief fund. All too often, somewhere between feeling that sense of *I should really do that* and actually doing it, the emotion loses momentum and you get distracted or think *maybe later*. Sadly, we find that emotions essential to Christian faithfulness like compassion, hope, and encouragement are especially difficult to sustain. Compassion so often gives out before we take all the needed steps to alleviate suffering in someone else's life (the action toward which compassion presses us), and hope and encouragement often fade before we have persevered through difficult seasons (which hope and encouragement are intended to gird us for). All too frequently our physical experience of the emotions that keep us pouring out our lives for our Lord sputter and quit on us before bearing behavioral fruit. Our bodies, it seems, are only too eager to stop fueling behaviors that cause discomfort, inconvenience, or sacrifice.

On the flip side, many emotions, especially fear and anger, have a habit of lingering in our veins long after the annoying comment from a coworker or the near miss with another vehicle on the highway is forgotten. We have all had the experience where our hearts were still pumping harder than normal an hour after some sudden fright, even though we were in no danger at all.

I (Alasdair) actually had this happen while working on this chapter. My wife and I were leaving our kids with her parents for two days while we took a long-anticipated two-day getaway. The actual handoff with the kids, however, was somewhat stressful;

I rushed out of work without neatening up my mind or my desk to meet Lauren, our kids, and her parents for an open house at our kids' school, where we raced from classroom to classroom, navigated meltdowns, and so on. After a few parting instructions to Lauren's parents (the macaroni and cheese is on the bottom shelf in the pantry; the pacifier is in the middle cabinet by the microwave; sorry we didn't get to the mess in the basement; and so on) we were finally on the road, headed to a nice dinner, breathing deeply and relaxing in freedom! At least, that's what I should have felt. Instead, I caught myself every three minutes or so driving too fast, hunched at the steering wheel, and tense in every muscle. By the fifth or sixth time I noticed what I was doing, checked myself, and slowed down, it dawned on me that, while there was no reason to hurry or stress, my body was stuck in the stress of the past few hours, and my heart was pounding away oblivious to my current situation.

While most of us will get over little incidents like this, as I did, in a matter of minutes or hours, some emotions can end up hanging around for months or even years like an awkward houseguest you can't persuade to move out. This is most common and most debilitating when it flows from some severe or traumatic life experience (the current name for this ancient human experience is post-traumatic stress disorder, or PTSD), where people find themselves still responding with full-throttle fight-or-flight reactions to triggers bearing any resemblance to the initial horrifying situation. Our bodies are all too easily trained.

In summary, when our emotions either drain too quickly or stagnate, our bodies hinder rather than help us in responding to our situations. And we are more reliant on the physical help from our bodies' emotions than we think.

Too Much or Too Little

The intensity with which our emotions come, regardless of how fast they come or how long they last, is important too. While we aren't suggesting that the strength or weakness of different people's emotions has a purely, or even primarily, biological cause, it's hard to deny that some people seem to feel their emotions in their bodies far more strongly than others do. However their emotions develop, some people find them sweeping into them like flash floods, while others experience hardly a ripple, even in response to significant events.

Let's look at the "too much" side of the spectrum first. Over-strong emotions tend to play out in two basic ways. Some people find their emotions constantly shifting; it's just that they hit hard when they hit. Intense anxiety might give way to towering rage and then plummet down into bleak despair in the course of an afternoon or even an hour, all triggered by a relatively minor incident. Again, many factors are at play, but it's significant that your body can become accustomed to spraying emotions out like a fire hose whenever the spigot opens at all.

At other times, however, instead of a fire hose, your heart can pour one steady, unrelenting color into your emotional paint bucket that drowns out all other streams of feeling, no matter how things shift around you. For example, if your thyroid gland malfunctions, your body will pour the physical experience of dark-purple depression into you, regardless of what is going on in your heart or circumstances. You may love Jesus or money or art history, but your physical energy and emotional buoyancy won't be lifted by successful evangelism, a big paycheck, or seeing Monet's *Haystacks at Sunset*.[2]

A more bizarre case of one's body getting stuck in a single emotion is mania. While bipolar disorder is complicated and far from fully understood, one way to conceptualize devastating manic episodes that wreak havoc is to say that mania essentially locks in a feeling of brash, even supreme, confidence. It's as if in mania your

---

2. An excellent resource on depression of every kind is Edward T. Welch, *Depression: Looking Up from the Stubborn Darkness*, originally published as *Depression: A Stubborn Darkness—Light for the Path* (Greensboro, NC: New Growth, 2004).

body is blaring out the message that nothing can go wrong and no plan your mind alights on could fail. This helps us understand why, in manic episodes, people so often take foolish risks, act out sexually, and spend ruinously irresponsible amounts of money. They seem unable to imagine that any of it could ever come back to haunt them. Their mania leaves them feeling, even physically, so sure of the goodness of their every desire that they go crashing through barricades and warning signs till they fly off the cliff and crash into bleak depression.

Just as emotions can come on too strongly, they can also come on too weakly. People can go numb over time, finding that neither joyful family events nor personal tragedies seem to have much impact on their moods. This is most common in people who would describe themselves as significantly depressed, but it can simply be a growing sense of withdrawal from the world or of burnout in the face of life's never-ending stresses.

Interestingly, gray numbness, with its loss of strong emotion, is a not-infrequent *side effect* of some antidepressants. It's as if the medication, in order to shield your body from falling into emotional sinkholes, condenses all your emotions toward the mundane middle of life's felt experiences. Many people do find that an antidepressant cuts out the devastating lows and are thankful for it, but they often find that unrestrained, full-belly-laugh happiness has been edited out as well.[3]

The bottom line is this: your body is constantly sending signals to your soul about how the world is going, and those messages become significantly problematic when they get pressed too hard, the glandular equivalent of a computer key getting stuuuuck in the down position. Equally problematic, however, are signals that don't activate at all, like a computer key that won't type when pressed.

---

3. This doesn't mean that taking antidepressants is a bad thing! Rather, it means what every psychoactive medication will tell you on the box: this isn't a miracle, and it may come with side effects. For many, the absence of incessant devastating lows is, for at least a time, a worthwhile trade-off for the loss of occasional elation.

Sometimes the Link Is Less Obvious

While it's helpful to think about where our emotions are clearly coming too fast, too long, or too hard, by far the most common negative physical-emotional feedback loops are even more mysterious, and the links between body, soul, and environment are even less clear. Panic attacks, ulcers, insomnia, and even tense shoulders fall into this category. Panic attacks, for example, can be brought on by specific events (being in a crowd, realizing you're lost, public speaking, etc.), but more often they hit at odd moments with no obvious trigger. Even when you can make a connection between a particular fear you had and your panic attack, it's still quite rare to identify the reason you went from feeling worried about something one day to having a panic attack about it the next. Our bodies simply seem to be in a feedback cycle with our hearts that shifts and ebbs unpredictably over time.

Let's make this a bit more accessible with a brief experiment. Take about fifteen seconds and do three things:

- Consciously relax your shoulders.
- Tilt your head slowly backward as far as you comfortably can.
- Take several deep breaths.

What did you notice? Did you find tension in your back, shoulders, neck, or chest? Were you consciously aware of the tension two minutes ago before you stopped and did this experiment? Did breathing and relaxing your muscles leave you feeling any different? For the vast majority of us, the back-and-forth between our bodies and our souls is happening in the background, and 99 percent of the time we don't notice it at all. Yet every moment we spend unconsciously tensed reinforces to our bodies subtly that our lives are stressful. Further, the natural result of your body endlessly telling you that life is stressful is a deepening cycle of your body becoming just that much tenser.

The list of mutual influences between your physical form and your feelings could go on and on. Operating on short sleep or being hungry makes it much easier to feel irritable. Drinking alcohol makes it somewhat easier to feel a number of things, including relaxation, happiness, depression, and reckless indifference. Dehydration places a small barrier between you and the feeling of contentment. Being tired or thirsty doesn't make it okay to be snippy or rude, of course, but it's helpful to recognize that too little sleep or water (or too many glasses of stronger drink) or a whole host of other physiological states and experiences will exert a steady pull on our emotions and thus become a source of trial and temptation in our lives.

A Very Brief Word on Brain Chemistry

You may have noticed that we have reached the middle of the fourth chapter of this book and yet have said next to nothing about what happens in the human brain when it experiences emotion. While this may have been a disappointment to you, it's been a very intentional choice on our part.

By saying so little about brain chemistry, we are not denying the impact of the body on our emotions; in fact we have emphasized taking the body into account! It is important, however, to recognize two things. First, while we both have a significant interest in the discoveries of brain research, neither of us has expertise in this area. We don't want to say more than we know.

Second, and more important, however, we live in a historical moment where the tendency is to overstate the role of the body. Thankfully, as a group, the actual scientists and cutting-edge researchers in psychology, psychiatry, and neuropsychiatry make appropriately restrained claims about the findings of their research. They are usually quick to acknowledge the limitations in what their studies have proven. Language like "our research *suggests*" and "it *may be the case* that certain neural pathways *play a significant role*" represents humility. We are thankful that many people are studying the human brain, one of God's most amazing creations; it is especially in the folds of our gray matter that God has mysteriously interwoven our souls and our flesh.[4]

We must remember though, that understanding the mechanics of the brain is *not* the same as understanding how to live rightly before the Lord. While it can help to know what's going on in your brain or glands, the deepest *whys* of your emotions are not the neural pathways they travel. Instead, the deepest *whys* are the things Scripture is constantly pointing to: the love and worship of your heart and your bearing the image of an emotional God. We were made to respond with love for what is good and hatred for what is evil. Our neural biology, then, which is so complex that it makes all the air traffic controllers in all the airports in the world look like a game of tic-tac-toe in comparison, is merely the stage on which we play out the moral drama of the universe.

On a practical level, this means you don't get angry because your adrenaline spiked, your serotonin levels dropped, your face flushed, and your breath quickened. On the contrary, your adrenaline spiked, your serotonin levels dropped, your face flushed, and your breath quickened because your good friend just criticized you in front of several other friends from church; and your whole body, from your sweat glands to the blood flow in the capillaries of your lungs, is pulsing with your desire to defend yourself. Your body is the vehicle through which the passion of your soul flows.

The basic point is this: no matter how much we come to understand about the biology of our brains, we will still always need

---

4. One particularly interesting recent example is the work of psychologist Lisa Feldman Barrett, *How Emotions Are Made: The Secret Life of the Brain* (New York: Houghton Mifflin Harcourt, 2017). She makes a strong case for emotions as "predictive," arguing that your brain actually builds your emotions based on a "guess" about the state of your body. She concludes that humans are far less rational than they'd like to think, and yet "you can take steps to influence your *future* emotional experiences, to sculpt who you will be tomorrow" (p. 176). Her suggested pathway to self-sculpting is by carefully controlling what you expose yourself to in life rather than by having the living God change the very loves of your heart in a real, two-way relationship. Even so, her careful study runs in the same direction as our thesis that growth in emotions demands change in who we are and what we love because these shape what we feel.

to wrestle with our emotions as expressions of what we love. While some people's bodies are much more sensitive to emotions than others, all of us experience the benefit (and the problem) of having our bodies stirred by the endlessly flowing stream of our emotions. At the core, dealing with difficult (or absent) emotions always comes back to growing in love for what God loves, hate for what God hates, and an ever-deepening relationship with God through every emotion.

This is good news! You don't have to have an advanced degree in neuroscience to grow in controlling anger, deepening compassion, grieving with hope, or finding joy in the midst of trials.

Your Body Matters, but It Can't Force You Away from God

We've just briefly skimmed over a few of the ways our bodies can affect the color of the emotions flowing into our paint buckets. Countless books and research articles have been written about the ways this plays out, and countless more will be. What we need to remember is that even when our bodies are influencing our emotions and confusing the mixture, it doesn't mean our hearts no longer matter or that the help of the living God and his Word have to take a back seat. It always makes a difference when we bring our hearts to him and receive his grace, even if that is the grace to endure one more day of our body flooding us with a flat-gray numbness. God delights in the faith and honor we show him when we seek to live in tune with his heart, no matter how turbulent or misguided our feelings may be.

Questions for Reflection

As you face your own feelings:

1. What do you notice about your own physical experience of emotions? Are your shoulders tight and tense right now?
2. Does the idea that your body can influence but not totally control your emotions relieve you? Does it discourage you? Why?

As you help others:

1. Are there people in your life who might need to see a doctor for a medical perspective on their stress, depression, grief, insomnia, or other condition related to their emotions?
2. Have you been influenced by the idea that our bodies control our emotions?
3. How has this chapter changed your perspective on helping people deal with their emotions?

5

You Relate to Others When You Feel with Them

What Does It Mean to Connect?

In chapter 2 we learned that one purpose of emotions is to help us relate or connect with each other. By "connecting" we mean sharing our hearts with one another in a deep and meaningful way.

Earlier I (Winston) described the day Kim and I bought our first home. It was a day of real ups and downs, elation and doubt, joy and anxiety. All of those emotions variously expressed what we valued—our hopes and dreams of building a family together as well as the fear that we had committed ourselves to jobs, bills, and a house that we couldn't easily escape. Our emotions broadcast loud and clear what was going on in our hearts. But the real connecting happened when we sat on the floor of our new home that night in near darkness under a single light and talked about what we were feeling. We listened to each other, and as we did we knew that the other understood and truly cared. It was a powerful, comforting moment in which we both knew we were loved. It wouldn't have been connecting if we had only privately noted the emotions of the other and kept going, or chided the other for the feelings he or she had. Connecting is more than simply knowing or observing how the other feels; it means entering into and personally engaging with the other's experience in a genuine and caring way.

The Image of the Body, "One Flesh"

Throughout the New Testament, Paul uses the human body to illustrate the nature of the church.[1] The members of the Corinthian church seemed to have an especially difficult time connecting with each other. They bickered over who should be their leaders and who had the greatest gifts and abilities, sued each other in court, and turned communion meals into drunken parties. Paul knew they needed a radically different way of thinking about what it means to relate to one another, so he challenged them to think of themselves as members of one body: "For just as the body is one and has many members, and all the members of the body, though many, are one body, so it is with Christ" (1 Cor. 12:12).

The idea is simply this: when God makes us one with Christ, he also makes us one with each other. Our physical bodies are made up of many different parts, each with different abilities and functions, all deeply connected as a unified body. We are connected to each other in the same way in Christ. We don't cease to exist as individuals, but we are deeply connected to one another just as we are deeply connected to Christ.

Paul has a lot to say about how Christ's body should operate, but one critical element is our obligation to connect with and care about each other's experiences. Paul writes, "If one member suffers, all suffer together; if one member is honored, all rejoice together" (1 Cor. 12:26; cf. Rom. 12:15). The observation is simple but profound. To relate to one another the way God wants us to means to be fully engaged in the experiences of the other. When the other is honored or is experiencing good things, you rejoice with that person. When the other is suffering or in pain, you feel the pain right along with the one suffering.

---

1. E.g., Rom. 12:4–8; Eph. 4:4–13; Col. 3:15.

Let the imagery of the body guide you. If you smash your finger in a drawer, you don't look down in curiosity at your finger and wonder: *That's odd. That finger seems to have been smashed in a drawer. I suppose that must really hurt . . . or does it?* No. You immediately connect with and respond to the pain. You yell, *"Ouch!"* (or something like that). You pull your hand from the drawer, hold that finger tightly, and rush to the sink and run cold water over it. You are "one flesh" with your finger. It may be small and seem unimportant, given its size, but when it's in trouble, your entire focus is on that finger, and you mobilize your entire body around its protection and care.

The Love Connection

Now, take what we have learned from your little finger and apply it to your relationships. When you are hurting, those most closely connected to you should respond, and vice versa. And when something good happens to you and you are happy, they should be happy right along with you, and vice versa. To be deeply connected means to enter into the experience of the other, to feel it right along with them, whether the feeling is good or bad. In fact, the Bible tells us that's a very basic function of love. That's why at the very end of everything Paul has to say about "the body," he writes what is sometimes called the "Love Chapter," 1 Corinthians 13, where he says:

> If I have prophetic powers, and understand all mysteries and all knowledge, and if I have all faith, so as to remove mountains, but have not love, I am nothing. If I give away all I have, and if I deliver up my body to be burned, but have not love, I gain nothing. . . .
> Love never ends. (vv. 2–3, 8)

All our abilities and all the ways we connect and relate are ultimately supposed to be expressions of love. Of course, this makes sense when we remember that it is Christ's body that we are talking about. After all, he is love incarnate. So we have to conclude that learning to use our emotions to connect is an important part of learning to love well.

How do you enter into someone's emotions? Here are a few suggestions. If you feel lost at sea in this whole conversation about emotions, you might start by simply cultivating curiosity about what people around you are feeling. You're much more likely to notice something when you're looking for it. When you do notice emotion or even a surprising change in someone—a usually boisterous friend is reserved and distant, a sibling seems flustered—slow down and ask questions about what's going on. Or, if questions don't seem appropriate or welcome, stop and put yourself in the other person's shoes and imagine what might make *you* feel that way. You may well be wrong about what others are feeling and why, but you at least are learning to put yourself in their shoes.

When you find yourself with a clear understanding of the emotion another person is experiencing, entering in is often as simple as choosing or allowing yourself to focus on that person. Nothing inhibits sharing someone's heart like a focus on oneself: *Am I being responsive enough? What are they thinking about me? Am I feeling as connected as I should be?* Invite others to talk about what they are feeling. As you listen, don't fight the discomfort of not being in control or able to make them feel different.

Remember that one purpose of emotions is to communicate what and how much things mean to us. You might say that our emotions are like relational price tags, communicating the value we place on things. The more we value something, the more we will experience emotions related to it. Back to the finger example: If you saw a stranger smash his finger in the drawer, you would probably wince and feel sympathy for him, but it would likely pass in a minute or two. If a good friend smashed his finger, you would feel it much more intensely. Your love for him would press you to come alongside him and assist him in determining how badly it was injured, maybe even drive him to the emergency room. The emotions that you experience about other people communicate what they mean to you. When they make you happy, sad, or angry, your emotions are expressing what and how much they mean to you.

Of course, exactly what our emotions are communicating can get complicated. For instance, intense anger can easily communicate contempt or hatred. And yet you may get very angry with someone in part because that person means a great deal to you. In fact, your love may be the very reason you are so upset about something this loved one has said or done. You would be much more upset at a close friend who lied to you, got drunk, and wrecked her mother's car than at a new acquaintance. C. S. Lewis perfectly captured the dynamic of our increased concern about destructive tendencies in those we love when he said that love "may forgive all infirmities and love still in spite of them: but love cannot cease to will their removal."[2] This means that sometimes being closely connected to another person will feel good, and sometimes it will feel bad. Either way, the point is that loving someone will always mean being touched emotionally by them.

That's why not sharing emotions in a relationship is a problem. No matter how deeply you love and are connected to someone, a lack of emotional expression and connection communicates a lack of love, which can have a subtle corrosive effect over time.

This doesn't mean everyone should or can express emotions in the same way. A high school boy might actually express more appreciation by punching a friend in the shoulder than a sixty-year-old woman would by greeting a tiresome relative with a peck on the cheek. A shy, reserved introvert may be sharing more openly in three brief sentences acknowledging a personal struggle than a boisterous extravert who talks for an hour about the highlights and lowlights of the week. The biblical goal of emotional connection is not that you follow a specific formula or phrasing;

---

2. C. S. Lewis, *The Problem of Pain* (San Francisco: HarperSanFrancisco, 1996), 39.

the goal is honest vulnerability about the things that are truly on your heart, and sincere interest in and empathy for the matters that excite or discourage your loved ones.

Having said that the format is not the important point, we should also say that it is often very important (and surprisingly difficult) to grow in speaking overtly about what you feel. The same holds for responding explicitly to the emotions you hear in others. In our marriage counseling, we see many couples in which one spouse complains of just not feeling loved. The other often responds with a lengthy list of evidence of true love shown to the first—helping to raise children, bringing income to the family, time spent together on vacations, gifts given, and so on. Almost invariably the root of the problem isn't with the list but with a lack of emotional connection, a failure to genuinely share experiences from the heart.

Imagine how you would feel if your spouse professed whole-hearted love for you and handed you a dozen roses or a new watch, but did it all in a mechanical voice and with a look of total disinterest. You would probably wonder if your spouse really meant it. In fact, you might justifiably suspect that something was very wrong. The actions and words would communicate love, but the tone and lack of emotional expression would communicate apathy or manipulation.

Emotions are not at the center of what love is, but they are a critical way of expressing it and connecting to others.

Practice Makes Perfect

Learning to connect with other people is a skill well worth learning. While emotional connection is not the only way we connect, this sharing of hearts and values and communicating a depth of care for others will be part of our delight for the rest of our lives, even our lives in heaven. All the images we have of heaven are of people sharing the joy of delighting in the King on his throne, singing together, expressing their collective passion for all he has done and who he is. This is exactly what we'd expect, given that God himself is a relationship—Father, Son, and Spirit—in which desires and delights are so mutually shared that Christ could rejoice in doing his Father's will even though it killed him.

Thus, while we are limited in our ability to understand these mysteries, we want every chance to connect heart to heart with another person to be an opportunity not just to grow more like the God who made us but also to grow in our awe that he would choose to share his heart with us. Our hope and promise is that each time we practice opening our hearts to someone, we are being made into the perfect likeness of Christ and are entering into his heart as well.

Questions for Reflection

As you face your own feelings:

1. Do you connect easily with others in their emotions? Why or why not?
2. What makes you feel most connected to others?

As you help others:

1. Do you find it hard to pick up on others' emotions? If so, do you think that cultivating curiosity about their emotions and making a special effort to pay attention to and ask about their feelings will help?
2. Are you overwhelmed by emotions in others? Why or why not? What do you do about it if you are?

6

Why Can't I Control My Emotions?

I (Alasdair) was frustrated with my wife. Okay, let's be honest—I was angry. I don't remember what the issue was or if we had even argued about it—sometimes my ugly silence is worse than a heated discussion. What I do remember is that it was after 11:00 p.m., and I was quite tired, but there wasn't a chance I was going to sleep anytime soon.

To make matters worse, while I can't now remember what the issue was, I *knew* even at the time I was mostly wrong. Maybe I had some fair points, but my self-pity and anger were definitely out of proportion with what had happened, and I couldn't deny it. Realizing that lying in bed and stewing wasn't going to get me anywhere, I got up, threw on a sweatshirt to ward off the New Hampshire evening chill, and slipped out for a walk. It was probably closer to pacing than walking, truth be told; my legs were trying to keep up with my racing thoughts.

I prayed: *Lord, you've got to help me. I'm trying. I just can't seem to stop feeling angry. Right now all I can think about is how unfair she was. I know I'm not loving her right now. I know I'm not where you want me. Help.*

Learning to pray like this, in the midst of seething internal frustration, represents massive growth for me. However, no sooner would I finish praying than thoughts about what *she* did to me leapt right back into my mind. It was as if a vivid documentary detailing the unfairness of her words and how she was the one at fault was playing on loop across the big screen in my head. The cycle of wrenching myself away from the documentary to pray and getting sucked back in repeated every thirty seconds or so as I marched through the darkness.

I'm not sure how many miles I covered, but I'll bet I was out there for two hours praying and rehashing, praying and rehashing. I took deep breaths. I kept my pace quick and my blood pumping. I tried to jar myself out of my distress by focusing my gaze upward on the few stars that sneaked past the night clouds.

Nothing worked. Tiptoeing back into the sleeping house I felt more or less the same as when I had slipped out.

I climbed back into bed in the early hours of that morning exhausted, as frustrated with myself as with my wife, hopeless that I would ever master the ugliness of my anger or self-pity.

———

Maybe you've never done laps around your block for hours at a time trying to fight yourself into feeling different, but you probably do know what it's like to hate the way you feel and yet find yourself unable to snap out of it. Anyone familiar with depression or anxiety certainly knows what it's like to be trapped in an emotion. Guilt, sadness, anger, numbness, envy, regret, despair, and bitterness can be formidable wrestling partners too—all capable of pinning you to the mat and sitting on your chest.

Why is this? Why do we so often feel like our emotions are controlling us rather than the other way round? Why can't we simply choose to feel different any time we want to?

Emotions Are Instinctive, and That Is a Good Thing

This is not a new question. Even some of the writers of the Bible experienced the frustration of trying to feel different but finding their emotions didn't come and go at their beck and call. The author of Psalm 42 provides us with one of the clearest examples. He famously writes that his soul "thirsts for God" like a "deer pants for flowing streams" (vv. 1–2). What is less well known is that he spends the rest of the psalm wrestling with his emotions, twice asking,

> Why are you cast down, O my soul,
>   and why are you in turmoil within me? (vv. 5, 11)

Even as he fights to remember the good things God has done and urges himself to hope in the Lord, his feelings seem to stay stuck, doggedly resisting his efforts to change them.

This lack of immediate change in the psalmist's feelings, however, doesn't mean his battle with his feelings is pointless. Nor does it mean he's fighting poorly. It simply means that he is human, and that the world around him must change at a significant level for his significant emotions to change. Rather than selecting our emotions on a whim off a menu of ways to feel, God gave us emotions that are actually *designed not to change* unless what we love changes or what is happening to the thing we love changes.

This is counterintuitive, so let's slow down for a moment with a pair of examples that demonstrate how good and natural it is that emotions overflow instinctively from our loves rather than resulting from conscious choices.

Your phone rings. It's your good friend from church who has been out of work for four months. She's calling to say that she got the new job in your department you'd both been praying she'd get. Now you'll be collaborating on projects weekly and talking in the break room every day. How do you feel? You are thrilled! Why? Because God made you to feel happy—let's-throw-a-party happy—*instantaneously*. You don't have to consult a spreadsheet of possible emotions and select "overjoyed" or "bubbling with excitement" as your mood of the moment. You love your friend, so news of her securing an income and spending more time with you yields immediate, reflexive elation.

While none of us are going to complain about good news bringing elation, you still see the basic point: it's normal and appropriate for emotions to come right away, without conscious choice. It would be odd if they required deliberation. Your friend would be hurt if she asked why you were silent after she told you her good news and you said, "I'm trying to decide how to feel about it."

Now take a second example: Your phone rings, but this time it wakes you up in the middle of the night, when phone calls always mean bad news. The worst news, in this case: your sister has been pulled from the wreckage of her car and is in a medevac chopper on the way to the nearest hospital. Her condition has stabilized and she is in and out of consciousness, but they aren't sure she'll make it. So you do what anyone would do: you sit down in your arm chair in the living room and think: *Hmm, how will I choose to feel about this? Gee, I could end up feeling anxious here, and I really don't like feeling anxious. I think I'll go with content and calm instead. Yes, that's the right choice. Ah, that feels so much better already. Now I'll make some coffee, finish that show I started before bed, and then get on over to the hospital.*

Of course not! Such a response would be unthinkable. Even if it were possible, it would be unspeakably selfish to putter about getting in your happy emotional zone and avoiding anxiety when you have the chance to maybe speak to your sister one last time on this earth. No, you are sprinting to the car before you can see straight from the sleep fog. Your anxiety is motivating you to rush to your sister, and that's as it should be. No amount of willpower is going to make you feel calm as you accelerate down the highway. Sure, on some level you might wish you didn't feel a terrible knot in the pit of your stomach or that your heart wasn't racing.

But on a more important level, the idea of feeling unfazed by such news should be repellant to us.[1]

The bottom line is simple: because emotions flow out of what we care about most, our emotions can't and shouldn't change apart from a change in what we care about (or a change in the wellbeing of what we care about).

Perfect Faith Doesn't Mean Control over Emotions

Now this leads us to an important nuance: we said a moment ago that "no amount of willpower is going to make you feel calm" racing to the hospital. But, you might ask, shouldn't it make a difference in my emotions if I am praying and trusting in God as I speed to the hospital? Shouldn't I be finding peace in his sovereign control?

This is a right and important question. The short answer is that it can and often does make a big difference to your emotions, even in moments of crisis, to remember that God is in control and that he is good. It can radically alter your emotional experience to talk with God in prayer about things that are troubling your heart. This question actually drives the entire middle section of this book. For now, we'll simply say that a vital, active relationship with a good and sovereign God matters a lot to your emotional life.

We Need New Hearts More Than New Feelings

We need to appreciate, however, that even when a relationship with God impacts your emotions, the *way* it does so is *not* by flattening them. Loving God more does not mean caring about others less! Instead, the way your relationship with God affects your emotions is by his Spirit constantly reshaping and refining what you love throughout your life (we treasure his kingdom and presence more as we mature, and our own kingdom and idols less).

---

1. While some people do experience a deep and pervasive numbness, which can extend even into situations like these, they are never thrilled to be numb, nor do they see the ability to be unaffected by tragedy as beneficial. Instead, they say things like "What's wrong with me that I am so disconnected?"

For this reason, part 2 of this book is *not* going to be full of tips for working directly on your emotions for the purpose of changing them. What it will do is give suggestions at many levels, including things you can do with body and mind, to participate with God in a process of ongoing heart change.

Unfortunately, this kind of heart-centered response to our emotions is rare. Our instincts run mostly in the opposite direction: reflexively we attempt either to change the emotions themselves or to escape from them. To control the situation or run from it. While no one can deny that control or escape can temporarily secure more comfortable emotions, it's the worship of our hearts rather than our emotions or our situations that most often needs changing.

Emotions are simply not meant to be turned off and on at will. They are meant to be dealt with at the source.

How Then Can I Change?

Scripture is adamant on this point: our biggest need is for new hearts with new loves and reoriented worship, not for more comfortable feelings. Deuteronomy, Jeremiah, and Ezekiel all underscore our need for hearts that are softened from stone, made clean, brought to life. Since we have seen how our love and worship produce our emotions, it makes sense that when our hearts are reshaped, our emotions follow suit. Of course, there will be complexity in the relationship between our treasures and our feelings beyond our ability to comprehend—especially where matters of the body are concerned, as we said in chapter 4. Of course we will all have to walk through dark seasons when our feelings of grief or anger don't and shouldn't change, those times when God is angry or grieved about the situation too. And of course, those who love God and his kingdom will rightly seek out his comfort in the midst of painful feelings about painful realities in a painful world. Nonetheless, our hope for change in our emotions should always be focused on the hope promised by God that he can change our hearts.

But this does not mean we should never take action in response to our emotions, nor that we are helpless to do anything about them! Instead, following the lead of the author of Psalm 42, we are called to deal effectively with our feelings on a daily basis. Learning to do this in concrete, practical ways will be the focus of the entire next part of this book.

Questions for Reflection

As you face your own feelings:

1. What feelings in your life right now would you change with the push of a button if you could? What do you think would happen, or how would your life be different? Can you imagine any value in facing and wrestling with these specific feelings?
2. As you prepare to move into part 2 of this book, take a little time now and write out your own answer to this question: How *should* emotions change?

As you help others:

1. Do you expect people to have control over their emotions and change them by force of will? If so, how does this shape the way you minister to others?
2. Do you expect people's emotions to be completely beyond their control, a reality of life they must take as a given? If so, how does this affect the way you minister to others?
3. If you haven't already, answer question 2, above.

PART 2

ENGAGING EMOTIONS

7

Two Pitfalls

We hope you are feeling greater clarity about how emotions work and how the things you love drive the feelings you have. As you've seen, we've been at great pains to capture the way that what you love fundamentally shapes what you feel.

But what if the things you love and treasure aren't good? What if you see problems or gaping holes in the value system of your heart? What should you do when you aren't sure what you are treasuring or why your emotions feel off?

Helping you respond with godly maturity to your emotions, good, bad, and ugly, is the goal of the entire middle part of this book.

As counterintuitive as it may sound, given the way we've been stressing the complexity of emotions, a biblical response to your emotions can actually be captured in a single word: *engage*. We are going to explain what we mean by that in chapters 8 and 9. First, however, you need to understand the two ways our culture, both secular and Christian, tends to drag us off the path God lays out for addressing our emotions well. This middle section of the book, then, begins by exposing the unhealthy views of dealing with our emotions that surround us (chap. 7). Then it lays out a biblical framework for healthy engagement with our emotions (chaps. 8–9). Finally, it closes with three broad categories of practical applications (chaps. 10–12).

So first things first: let's start by recognizing and critiquing the problematic ideas in the cultural air we breathe.

"Spit It Up"—Emotions Are Everything

The loudest voice in the room, at least in the Western world, tells us that our emotions are everything, the most important thing, the thing that most defines us. Perhaps few would say it that bluntly, but expressions of this belief are all around us. This doesn't mean our culture assumes that you understand your feelings or where they come from, or that you even like your emotions. Fundamentally, however, you live among a people whose actions and cultural practice proclaim over and over again that *what you feel is the most important thing about you.*

Now when we say "the most important thing," we obviously don't mean that our society thinks your experience of emotion is more important than your intake of oxygen. Instead, we simply mean that the highest good our culture seeks for living, breathing individuals is having good feelings. It means that, in our culture, a problem with one's feelings is one's biggest problem. It means the greatest harm you can do to someone is not to listen to, give space for, and affirm what that individual *feels* is needed to *feel* the way he or she wants to *feel*. Hence the extreme value placed on "authenticity" (Google pulls up more than two hundred million hits for it). Hence the embrace of sexuality as the core of human identity. Hence emphasis on instilling self-esteem. Hence, as one church historian has put it, the shift in the American church from "salvation to self-actualization."[1]

Given this starting point, the next step the culture takes is quite natural. If the most important thing about you is your feelings, then you need to be and express yourself at pretty much all

---

1. E. Brooks Holifield, *A History of Pastoral Care in America: From Salvation to Self-Actualization* (Nashville: Abingdon, 1983).

costs. This is why we value "getting it off your chest," "letting off steam," "just being honest," "saying what you feel," and so on. It also can lead to a host of actions that I "have to" take because a situation is "making me" feel bad. Thus, we might pull back from a friendship that makes us feel bad about ourselves, or do community service to feel good about ourselves. Either way, the end goal is how we feel.

In short, it's like we live in an airport terminal with a loud-speaker blaring over the babble of all the other conversations, informing us that our feelings are the most important thing in the room. We are instructed to handle this fragile baggage by expressing our emotions to the fullest (no matter what others may think) or rearranging the furniture around us to make space for them (we applaud the courage of those who refuse to silently accept the world as it is).

Now think about this cultural assumption for a moment. Are your emotions really the *most* important thing about you? We're writing a whole book on emotions, so obviously we do think they are important! Further, we're going to spend significant time arguing for the value of talking about your emotions with God and others. But to place your feelings ahead of the quality of your character, ahead of the faithfulness of your obedience to God, ahead of the depth of your relationships with God and others—even to place your feelings ahead of the feelings of others—is the *opposite* of what Scripture calls us to!

This issue is not a purely secular problem. The church has its own versions of this broader cultural value. Often, for example, we elevate our emotional experience to the peak of Sunday morning worship. The goal of the sermon is to *feel* deeply convicted or inspired; the goal of the music is to *feel* a rush of ecstasy or thanksgiving; the goal of coffee hour is to *feel* connected and included. This mentality often drives personal devotions as well; the point is to have a dramatic emotional experience of seeing Jesus's beauty, or to have less anxiety, or to feel closer to God.

Again, please hear us carefully. These feeling are wonderful things in themselves! We ought to earnestly seek experiences of God through his Word and his people, and rejoice when sermons or songs move our hearts. But it's so easy for a healthy appreciation of emotion in our spiritual experience to slide over into an unhealthy emotionalism that begins to make the emotion itself the point. Far too many of us can resonate with a woman who told us, "I felt an endless pressure at church to reach the next level, to have the next great emotional experience. It was exhausting."

To be fair, this placing of emotions on a pedestal does get three important things right. First, your emotions really do tell you something important about who you are. To use our language from chapter 2, our culture understands that our emotions communicate. Second, as we said in chapter 6, it's true that our emotions cannot be perfectly controlled by simple willpower, and, even if they could be, restraining them should not be our default response. Finally, as we'll discuss more in chapters 8 and 9, we are glad our culture places value on giving voice to the things inside us, even when that isn't comfortable for us or those around us.

But these valid insights are at best half the story. Our culture's overemphasis on the role of emotions constantly trains us to be ruled by our emotions. This, in turn, inevitably slides toward an increasingly frantic pursuit of emotional highs and escaping from emotional lows. Such an approach leans away from the richer and ultimately more satisfying "long obedience in the same direction" as Eugene Peterson, a Christian author and thinker, once described the Christian life.[2] Just as cookies are a terrible nutritional center for your diet, so emotions make a terrible *central* priority for your life.

"Suck It Up"—Emotions Are Nothing

Perhaps it won't surprise you to learn that there is a second, opposite instinct out there. This instinct holds that emotions ought

2. From Eugene H. Peterson, *A Long Obedience in the Same Direction: Discipleship in an Instant Society* (Downers Grove, IL: InterVarsity Press, 1980).

to be treated like a stray rabid dog that has wandered into your living room. Call it keeping a stiff upper lip, stoicism, or being a tough guy, the second voice from our culture argues (albeit more quietly than the first) that emotions are not to be trusted. And, given the way our culture's worship of emotion often encourages people to pit their feelings against truth or obedience, it's not hard to understand why this stoic minority reaction has been especially popular in many Christian circles.

The classic image of the "suck it up" perspective on emotions is the Marlboro man, or any dirty, sweating, blood-spattered hero from an action movie. The cattle may be straying, the bad guys may be showering his position with a hail of gunfire, and he may have just lost his best friend, but he won't be stopped. The modern, slightly more sensitive version of this hero will even have a tear in the corner of his eye for a lost buddy before he turns and charges into the teeth of the fray, but the implicit message is clear: strong, independent men are radically in control of their emotions. When our hero does express emotion, it is usually stiff-lipped, momentary silence, and he never lets his emotions stop him from doing what "oughta" be done.

All the images in the paragraph above are men, but the strong silent type increasingly has its female form too. Further, moving beyond over-the-top summer blockbusters into real life, the most significant rising star in the therapeutic world these days, mindfulness, actually has some stoic tendencies. This isn't surprising, given that mindfulness stems from Zen Buddhist practice, which emphasizes the need to deal with the suffering of the world by emotionally distancing oneself from it. While few Western therapists would use mindfulness with any connection to its Eastern roots, the mindfulness that has become so popular everywhere, from schools to clinical treatment centers, does still have stepping back from one's emotions as a central tenet. Presumably part of its popularity derives from the way mindfulness effectively pushes back against the dominant narrative of emotions-are-everything, which leaves people with no easy way to guard against the flood of emotions they feel. While we believe that the Bible offers something richer than mindfulness practices, our goal in raising the issue of mindfulness is not actually to critique it (or commend it). We are simply pointing out that, even in this emotion-worshiping culture, the hottest strategy for emotional self-regulation right now is actually on the stoic side of the spectrum.

Just as the church struggles with overvaluing emotions, so too the church has its own version of stoicism. Christian stiff-upper-lip-ism tends toward the kind of problems we highlighted in chapter 1, where one immediately repents of any negative emotion in oneself and rebukes it in others. The driving theological idea here is that negative emotions are inappropriate, given God's sovereignty. If God ordained this suffering to happen and he works all things for good, then the only reason to feel bad is if you don't have enough faith.

The experience of one particular woman in her early thirties captures this problem all too well. This woman lived through one of the most horrible evils a person can ever undergo—she lost her child. Her daughter, an only child conceived after significant difficulty, died at two and a half years from cancer. While many in her church expressed sorrow and compassion, she talked about being pressured to "be in church the very next Sunday, with a smile on so that everyone could see how good God is when life is hard." Was she exaggerating the attitude others had toward her? Perhaps. We hope so. But even if she heard an exaggerated version, this kind of thinking is quite common, and there is no reason to doubt she was perceiving an accurate core mentality.

Now, we have both personally experienced the blessing of being in church in the midst of grief. There is nothing quite like being known, cared for, and supported, and tasting God's mercy and goodness through the fellowship of his people in the face of loss. Yet this woman's experience was not of church as a place of comfort in her anguish. Instead, church was a place where only good emotions are allowed, and the goal in tragedy is to show that faith conquers negative emotions. We wish stories like this were the extreme exception, a distant statistical outlier. Sadly, this woman was tapping into something all too common, even if it isn't always so blatant.

The great tragedy here is that this kind of thinking warps God's sovereign control over every atom in the universe and every event, even the terrible death of a child, a control that truly is the bedrock of all our hope in the face of suffering, evil, and calamity that we don't understand. It's true that the stoic end of the spectrum may rightly perceive something vital about God's power and radical commitment to bringing good out of even the most hideous situations. Further, it's also true that we are not meant to be enslaved by our emotions. However, stoicism misses that emotions are a God-given gift, an aid in obedience, a constant occasion for connection with the Lord, and a vital source of information about the deeper problems of our hearts. Even the most problematic emotions are never the *true* problem. The true problem is the collection of warped loves of our hearts and the shattering of God's good creation. Instead of fighting dark feelings simply because they feel bad, we must carve out room in our theology for sadness, fear, anger, guilt, shame, dismay, and the like. Without them our faith becomes lopsided, a car with wheels on only one side, grinding and scraping along, veering constantly off the road God's Word would keep us on.

Thus, while we can sympathize with elements of both the hyper-emotionalism and the stoicism around us, we must reject the oversimplification both of these options represent. We need a third way, a way that takes our emotions seriously without handing them the keys to our lives. Chapters 8 and 9 seek to give a framework for that third way.

Questions for Reflection

As you face your own feelings:

1. Do you tend more toward the feelings-at-center-stage side or toward the just-get-over-it side of dealing with your emotions?

2. What about the group(s) with whom you spend most of your time? Where are hyper-emotionalism and stoicism exerting their influences on you from the outside?

As you help others:

1. Have you ever been the person who used God's sovereignty as a club to tell hurting individuals they should stop hurting? Is it too late to seek their forgiveness, or maybe even bring comfort?

2. Have you ever encouraged someone to put emotions at the center of his or her life, maybe implying that God basically exists to meet everyone's emotional needs? Is it too late to seek forgiveness, or maybe even offer a different perspective?

3. Most people you help are struggling with both pitfalls—in different ways—simultaneously. Can you identify areas where either or both are at play?

8

Engage: A Better Option

As we said in the last chapter, we think the word *engage* best captures the balanced approach of Scripture to the unbalanced extremes the world around us suggests for dealing with our emotions. Engaging walks a deliberate, middle road between the twin pitfalls of the hyper-emotionalism that fawns over our feelings and sets them up as dictators and the stoicism that squashes negative emotions from the outset. The Bible's model of *engaging* emotions means something very simple: when an emotion comes on your radar, you look at it, see what you find, and *then* (not before!) decide how to respond.

The beauty of engaging is that it doesn't judge your emotions ahead of time as either good or bad. When you engage something, you move closer and explore it, preparing yourself to deal with whatever you uncover. If, as we have argued thus far, there are good negative emotions (as well as bad) and bad positive emotions (as well as good), then it is imperative that we figure out what is going on before working to shut down or amplify the feelings flowing from our hearts.

We're more used to this kind of approach in dealing with our thoughts and actions than we are in dealing with our emotions. We all know that we all have good behavior and bad behavior, good thinking and bad thinking. But treating joy *and* anger as both potential threats and potential friends is less natural.

How then can you engage your elusive emotions? Here are four steps:

Identify

The first step can sound so basic as to be not worth mentioning: to engage something, you need to become aware that it exists and put a name of some sort on it. This, however, is actually the hardest step for many! For obvious reasons, coming to the conscious realization that you are in fact feeling something and then putting some kind of descriptive words on that feeling is quite challenging for someone who hasn't realized he or she is feeling anything at all. For some of us, being asked, "Why are you so upset?" or "How do you feel about that?" is like being blind and having someone ask you what color the sky is today. If this is you, turn to someone you trust and ask, "What emotions do you see in me most often? What do they look like when I show them?"

Now, when we say "name" what you are feeling, we don't mean you need a specific label or even a name that sounds like an emotion. "I'm feeling off" or "something's up" or "I am feeling something I can't explain and I don't know why" would be a perfectly valid way of identifying emotion. The point in this first step is simply to become aware that something is occurring inside you. You can only engage something effectively once you know it is there.

This is nothing magical or novel. You are simply trying to describe your reaction to the world God has put you in, using the words God has given. This is what the Bible does constantly. Thus the Gospels tell us that Jesus was "sorrowful and troubled" as his death approached (Matt. 26:37), or thankful to his Father for making the gospel accessible to even little children (Luke 10:21). And thus the psalmists tell us, "My heart is struck down like grass and has withered" (Ps. 102:4), or "I am weary with my crying out" (Ps. 69:3), or "I will be glad and exult in you" (Ps. 9:2). Gideon trembles with fear and asks for a fleece. Mary trembles too and asks why God has chosen her, and so on. Why the psalmist is sick at heart or what Jesus does with his deeply troubled spirit remains to be seen. For now, all we need to do is notice that Scripture's first step in engaging emotions in the people it talks about is simply to identify their feelings.

Examine

Once you've observed that an emotion is present, the next step is not rocket science: look at it, turn it around, and see what you can learn about it. Here we pull the categories of "communicate," "relate," "motivate," and "elevate" back into service (see chap. 2). Your emotions are always telling you something about what you are valuing, caring about, or loving. What are they telling you? They are always saying something about your relationships. What are they saying? They are always pressing you toward some kind of action. What are they energizing you to do? Finally, they are always influencing your relationship with God. What is their effect on your worship right now? In other words, examining emotions entails asking questions like *Why am I feeling this? What am I reacting to? Why is this hitting me so hard? Why isn't this affecting me the way it usually does?* and *How is this emotion making me want to behave?*

Let's look at a hypothetical example. Suppose you identify that you are feeling angry. As you examine your anger, you observe that you are mad about your wife breaking the lawn mower. When you first found out, you didn't say anything, but you've been curt since and weren't very talkative at dinner. Inside you keep thinking, *She knows I always get to the lawn on Saturday; why couldn't she just leave it alone?*

What can you learn about yourself from this? Here are a few possibilities. First, your anger is leading you to pull back (talking less than normal and less warmly than normal). Second, your emotion is leading to strain between you and your wife. Third, you value efficiency and comfort. Losing (you'd probably call it "wasting") time or money on fixing the lawn mower pulls time and money away from other things you had wanted to accomplish or enjoy. If this is true, it makes you one of about 7 billion people on the planet who value having things go smoothly! Your anger is identifying this setback as a bad thing that should not have happened. Lastly, however, the frustrated thoughts running on loop in your head suggest that right now you care more about the inconvenience to you than the good intentions your wife showed in doing something to make your life better. You're more concerned with the outcome than with her motives.

This might seem obvious, but it's important to recognize that the same situation could go very differently. For example, your anger at her could be from feeling insulted—she must not think you are man enough to do your own yard work. Or you could have been angry with yourself for not getting to the lawn last weekend and creating a situation where she felt she had to. You could be angry because, yet again, she didn't ask how to do something before jumping into a project; or you could be angry with her for not asking because she always asks, and this inconvenience wouldn't have happened if she'd stuck to the script. You could be angry at the lawn mower's manufacturer, who designed such a fragile product.

Those are just different options for what your anger might mean, but of course your response might have been something besides anger altogether! You could have felt fear; and, instead of anger leading to annoyed withdrawal, you might have placated her because you didn't want her to get upset with you or the situation and make life miserable. Or you could have felt joy that, after some recent conflicts between you, she took initiative and did something to bless you and didn't ask for help because she wanted it to be a surprise. A hundred bucks at the small-engine repair shop? A small price to pay for such a gift.

The list of possible reasons for feeling angry or afraid or joyful in a situation is endless. For our purposes, as you examine yourself, you aren't interested yet in whether what you're seeing is good or bad; you're just trying to understand what is going on. Whether what you see is a problem or not, you want to become as aware as possible of what you are caring about, how you are relating, and what you are doing in response.

Evaluate

Once you have identified that something is happening inside you and examined what is going on in that feeling, you're ready to take the next logical step: figuring which aspects of what you are feeling are good and godly and which are destructive or selfish. This is hard to do! You will rarely find only good in your emotions or only bad. Instead, you'll almost always find good and bad mixed together. And you have a lot at stake; you wouldn't be feeling emotion about it if you didn't.

How might our husband with the tall grass and the helpful-if-not-mechanically-savvy wife evaluate his anger? He certainly doesn't need to feel bad about his desire to use his Saturday efficiently or his hope that machines will work. Part of human suffering since Adam and Eve sinned is that our labor is beset by thorny setbacks, breakdowns, and obstacles. The Bible calls this a "curse," not a necessary part of the circle of life, and we are right to feel anger toward the broken, plan-thwarting consequences of living in a world warped by the presence of evil. God actually uses the frustrations in our work to remind us of the pervasive poisoning impact of sin and to leave us longing for the return of his Son to restore all things. Anger at a broken lawn mower can be part of a hunger and thirst for the courts of the Lord!

That said, when freedom from inconvenience is driving a man's reaction, rather than appreciation for his wife's efforts to help, something is off. A good desire has gone sour because it has gotten out of order in the priority scheme. When anger at a broken world turns into curt withdrawal, a punishment meted out on a well-meaning wife, it loses its Godward momentum and exacerbates the curse just a little bit more.

Our God calls us to love what he loves and hate what he hates. Few things bring more joy to God's heart than acts of premeditated, self-sacrificing love for each other. We were made to give and receive love just as Father, Son, and Spirit treasure, honor, and glorify each other. To ignore or be unmoved by a wife's thoughtful, personal kindness points to a self-absorbed and entitled heart. Sadly, every last one of us acts out of self-absorption and entitlement all too often.

The bottom line then in evaluating emotions is this: it's okay to be upset about what upsets God, and glad about what makes him happy. But when you find yourself ignoring what pleases him (e.g., the wife's intentions) and acting in ways that anger him, you need to evaluate your emotions as revealing something wrong in your heart.

Act

When you know *that* you are feeling, have named *what* you are feeling as best you can, and have decided *which* aspects of the feeling are good and which are bad, you are finally ready to act. While options for action are endless, proper responses to emotions fall into two fundamental categories.

On the one hand, we want to embrace and nurture the loves of our heart and the behaviors that are good. On the other hand, we want to resist and even starve loves and actions that are bad.

Remember, this does not mean focusing primarily on changing the emotions themselves! Changing your feelings is *not* your biggest goal. Instead, we want to let our evaluation of our emotions drive us to act in ways that will actually have an impact on the deep loves and treasures of our hearts. Thus, we will spend the next three chapters looking at various options for nourishing or starving the good or bad loves underlying our emotions.

To give you an idea of where we are heading, let's turn back to our angry husband one final time and think about what he should do. First, it's completely fair for him to pray that the lawn mower will be fixed easily and cheaply. Second, it would actually be *good* for him to express his frustration with broken equipment to God and voice his disappointment about the negative impact on his Saturday. After that, however, his examination and evaluation should show him that his heart is in the wrong place, caring more about his comfort and convenience than about his wife's love for him or spiritual growth. We want that realization to lead him to honest repentance in conversation with God about the problem in his heart this self-examination has uncovered.

Finally, while he may need a few minutes to cool down, he needs to talk to his wife. All the internal self-awareness in the world doesn't help if it doesn't lead to change in relationship and action. He needs to begin by apologizing to her for being short. He may want to reassure her that it's going to be okay. He should surely thank her for trying to take care of something for him. There may even be a place for him to make a gentle request that she get his input on lawn equipment in the future. Looking slightly further down the road, this could actually be a great opportunity for some ongoing, targeted Bible study (seeking help from friends or a pastor if he is at a loss for where to turn in Scripture) to prod and press his heart toward valuing things that will last into eternity (his wife's love) more than things that will pass away (money, time, and mowed lawns).

A Thousand Ways to Engage

Our hope is that you don't find this overwhelming. It certainly could be overwhelming to think of all the different meanings our feelings can have and all the different ways we might need to respond. One of the great joys of our faith, however, is that so many different practical, concrete responses to the things we find in our hearts can express faith. God has given us a shocking amount of leeway in living out our faith—there are so many right actions and right ways to nurture what is good (and starve what is bad)! The more we understand the connection between our situation, our emotions, and our loves, the better we will be able to creatively and consistently bear fruit in engaging our feelings.

But, before we start to explore the thousand ways to cultivate healthy hearts, there is one vital piece of the puzzle that needs its own chapter. Without this piece the whole picture falls apart.

Questions for Reflection

As you face your own feelings:

1. Is this making any sense?
2. Which step is hardest for you: identify, examine, evaluate, or act?

As you help others:

1. How might you help someone identify emotions in himself or herself that he or she can't see? If the person you are walking with asked you, "What emotions do I feel most often, from what you've seen?" what would you say?
2. When you think about evaluating someone else's emotions, do you find yourself immediately searching for an idol to tear down? It's tempting to "help" others by saying, "Here's what's wrong; just change this and you'll be okay."

9

Engaging Emotions
Means Engaging God

It's usually considered bad form to point out flaws in your writing. But we left a gaping hole in what we said about engaging our emotions in the last chapter, and it is absolutely vital that we fill the hole.

Did you catch what was missing? Taking our emotions to God got left off the list of steps!

We left prayer out of the four steps of engaging emotions for a very good reason though: engaging God in your emotions and about your emotions is not a step in a process! Instead, every single nuance of every aspect of each step must involve engaging God as well. Engaging our emotions does indeed mean identifying, examining, evaluating, and acting, but engaging our emotions also means engaging the One who made them.

Engaging emotions without engaging God is a recipe for disaster.

Our emotions are fundamentally designed to force us to engage him, and the great lie—which, ironically, both stoicism and hyper-emotionalism buy into—is that we can and should deal with our emotions apart from bringing them to the Lord. If we don't engage God but simply use a "Bible-based system" or "method" of handling our emotions, we lose the core hope we have as Christians. That hope is not in a system of strategies we can enact (though we are grateful for an action plan!) but in a Savior and Shepherd and ever-present help in time of need who sees us, knows us, loves us, and actually has the power, right here and right now, to help us with the turmoil of our hearts.

Let's see if we can slow down and catch the scent of this in Scripture.

Engaging God Means Pouring Your Heart Out

Engaging God in our emotions is quite simple (even if it can be exceedingly difficult to bring ourselves to actually do it). Psalm 62:8 captures it with profound simplicity:

> Trust in him at all times, O people;
>> pour out your heart before him;
>> God is a refuge for us.

If you trust God, David tells us, then *pour out your heart* to him. Or, put another way, trusting God necessarily includes pouring your heart out to him.

What does it mean to "pour out your heart"? The metaphor actually works nicely with our emotional paint-bucket analogy from chapter 3 (p. 46). Pouring out your heart simply means naming the colors you feel most strongly. It means bringing the sloshing mixture of churning paints to God and upending it into his hands one sentence at a time.

This is really quite a shocking thing for God to invite and even command us to do. Why would God be willing, much less eager, to hear the inner distresses and delights of people who from birth have rebelled against him? Why would God want hearts poured out into his hands when those hearts are divided, full of treasures that compete with single-minded devotion to him? Why would God choose to care about or listen to the weeping or pleading or crowing of a sinful creature who caused his beloved Son to go through physical and emotional anguish we could never fathom?

Would you offer your shoulder to cry on to someone who killed your child?

We need to press this point. All of us are easily presumptuous, blind to the privilege offered us in God's call to pour out our hearts. Imagine, the Father himself cares what you think, invites you to earnest conversation with him at any time, for as long as you need. A stunning honor—and yet we mostly see prayer as a tiresome duty. (Even the familiarity of the term *prayer* can work against us.) It doesn't occur to us most of the time that prayer can and should include simply talking to God about what is on our hearts.

Yet this is exactly what we observe over and over in the Psalms.

Too often, even taking the time to ask in prayer for God to help us or do things for us feels inconvenient and impractical. *How much more inefficient*, we think to ourselves, *to do nothing but blabber on in prayer about one's feelings!* Yet, in his mercy, God chooses to offer his listening ear to us, drawing out the depths of our soul in the safety of relationship with him.

We need to be brought up short by the shocking gift of pouring out our hearts to God.

The importance of emotions in our relationship with God shouldn't really surprise us. As we said in chapter 5, relationships need emotions like fires need oxygen. It stands to reason, then, that if our emotions are the way our hearts were made to align with God's, our relationship with him actually ought to be the most emotional relationship we have.

Fundamentally, God gave you emotions to connect you, bind you, and draw you to himself. To engage your emotions in any other way than by bringing them to him goes against the very grain of your human, image-bearing nature. Is it possible for human beings to make significant changes to their motives and feelings through willpower, creativity, sheer grit, dumb luck, or self-effort, without any reference to the God who made us? Yes. Because God made us with the power to have real impact on our world and ourselves, and because of God's mercy on us, even people who don't believe he exists can do things that cause their emotions to run in paths they prefer. But for your feelings to reflect God's feelings about this world and all that happens in it, you must bring your feelings to him. Trying to develop a heart whose emotions overflow from loving what God loves without bringing your feelings to him is like trying to fly by flapping your arms instead of boarding an airplane.

Who You're Engaging Matters

Psalm 62 says one more very important thing we haven't mentioned yet. It doesn't end with the command to trust God by pouring out your heart. It ends by telling you *why* you can pour out your heart and *why* you can trust him.

God is your *refuge*.

It is hard to overstate the emphasis Scripture places on this point. Countless verses echo the words of Psalm 71:3,

> Be to me a rock of refuge,
>> to which I may *continually* come.

Unless you know God is trustworthy, you won't entrust yourself to him, especially not the precious treasures of your inmost heart. Only a God who promises to hear you and who really will handle the fragile affections of your soul with tenderness inspires the necessary confidence in us to lay our loves into his hands. It is because David knows how deeply we all struggle to trust God with the things we really care about that he emphasizes that God is a refuge when he calls us to bare our hearts.

Scripture is full of similar promises. Why does Peter speak of "casting all your anxieties on him" (1 Pet. 5:7)? Because, Peter tells us in the simplest of words, "he *cares* for you." Do you realize what it means to care for someone? To devote time and energy and thought and effort to what will be good for another person and then act on that because you feel deep concern and affection for him or her. Or, when the author of Hebrews encourages us to come confidently to God's throne with our needs for sustenance and mercy, notice that he begins by reassuring us that Jesus can sympathize with us in our weakness and frailty (Heb. 4:15–16). God, the author of Hebrews wants us to know, is both strong enough and close enough to handle our most fragile treasures.

The Bible will not compromise on this point: we really can trust God. We have every reason to believe he is utterly committed to doing good to us and that he is more trustworthy in caring for us than we are in caring for ourselves. And we need every bit of it if we are going to pour out our hearts to him. It's all too instinctive for us to remain distant, disappointed, or demanding and, as a result, to pull back and keep our hearts to ourselves.

Even Jesus Did This

Did Jesus take his emotions to God? Did he need to? If Jesus's loves were perfect, then his emotions were perfect too. Doesn't it seem like he shouldn't have needed to bother with praying them?

Yet pray them he did.

Let's start with the most vivid example: the garden of Gethsemane. When Jesus says, "My soul is very sorrowful, even to death" (Matt. 26:38), what does he do? He doesn't pull out an extra bottle of wine from the Last Supper and take the edge off. He doesn't stand apart from his emotions to get some distance and seek to return to the calmness of his wise mind. He doesn't even start reciting his favorite Bible verses and preach truth to himself so he can stay focused on doing the next task for God. Instead, he does two simple, relational things. He speaks honestly to his friends about the dread and ache he is feeling as he anticipates the coming twenty-four hours. (In some ways his choice to invite sinful humans into his emotions and ask their help in prayer is even more shocking than his need to bring his feelings to his Father!) Then, having asked for help from his disciples, he falls on his knees and pours out his heart to his Father, just as Psalm 62 urges.

What did it sound like? He didn't rail in anger or bargain. Instead, the cries that echoed through the trees to his disciples that night were the stuff of pure relationship and profound trust. In the simplest terms, Jesus put his heart, his pain, his hopes, and his horrified anticipation of agony in utterly trustworthy hands.

The earnest tears of Gethsemane are the signature proof that our emotions, no matter how dark, are to be a door braced open between our innermost hearts and our Father's throne room. If Jesus brought to his Father his desperate sorrow and urgent desire for a way out, how can we not also bring to our Father our muddled loves and the mixed feelings they produce?

Once you see Jesus's engaging God in his emotions in the garden, you begin to see it everywhere. He engages God even in the unimaginable separation that takes place on the cross, using the words of Psalm 22:1 "My God, my God, why have you forsaken me?" He turns to his Father in Luke 10:21 and expresses joy that God brings the weak and lowly into the kingdom, setting a bar so low that even little children can enter (and the proud stumble over it). Are you beginning to see how Jesus's frequent retreats to quiet places in the early morning and his staying behind after dismissing a crowd so he could spend a night praying on a mountainside are more than the diligent practices of dutiful ritual but rather the lifeblood of his ministry? Jesus actually *needed* to pray. He needed to bring his heart to his Father, to pour out his concerns—for himself, for those he loved, and for his mission—into the only ears that truly understand all, the only hands that can truly help.

Walk through the Door . . . Constantly

If one of the core purposes of our emotions is to drive us to pour our hearts out to God, and if even Jesus needed to pour out his heart to God, why is walking through the open door toward God so hard for us? Several reasons spring to mind, but they are all variations on one central theme: we don't (fully) trust him.

But you will trust something. You *will* take your emotions to someone.

At the end of the day, the only reason we ever fail to dash toward the Lord with any of our emotions is that we aren't completely convinced it is worth it.

The most common reason we escort our emotions elsewhere is that it never occurs to us to take them to God. We don't trust him with our emotions because he seems irrelevant, or we assume we ought to get our act together before going to him. Many of us, even those of us who read our Bibles every morning, act as if our formal devotional time is the only slice of our day when we should or could interact with God.

Sometimes we hold back for more dramatic reasons. Many fear that God is against them. Even when things are going somewhat smoothly, they wait anxiously for the other shoe to drop. Others describe a deep sense that they are second-class citizens in the kingdom; surely if God really cared for them, he would give them the wife, the job, the financial security, or the friendships he seems to bestow so liberally on everyone else. Still others envy the closeness and ease with which certain acquaintances seem to approach God, and quietly question why their own spiritual walk is so drab and dry.

If you identify with these more "dramatic" difficulties, let us offer a word of encouragement before we move on. While you see greater problems in your walk with God than someone who doesn't think to pray outside his daily devotional slot, there is actually a way in which you are in much better shape. You're aware you have a problem! Only those who know they need medicine bother to see a doctor.

Why is it such a big deal to bring your emotions constantly to God? Can he truly be asking us for even more than devotions in the morning, integrity in our business dealings, and refraining from yelling at the kids?

It is a big deal to bring your emotions to God because reading your Bible, doing honest business, and keeping your cool as a parent are not the end goal of human life. Loving the Lord and walking with him is.

I (Alasdair) recently had a man I counseled chide himself for not having his devotions frequently enough. He commented that the "good stuff," meaning doing personal Bible study, wasn't going to happen "between 8:00 a.m. and 6:00 p.m.," when he was at work. While I appreciated the high value he placed on daily devotions, I came back at my friend strongly: "The good stuff is exactly what happens between eight and six. That's the whole point of *having* devotions!"

> He has told you, O man, what is good; . . .
> to do justice, and to love kindness,
>   and to walk humbly with your God. (Mic. 6:8)

Walking with God, for however many heartbeats, birthdays, and cups of coffee he gives you—that's the good stuff. Nothing is more natural than to talk candidly with a trusted friend as you walk side by side. Nothing is humbler or more just and upright or more fitting in response to the merciful invitation of the living God than to pour out your heart to him.

The "good stuff," then, is a narrowly avoided accident on the highway when you turn to God, your heart still hammering, with a jumble of "That was really, really close!" and "Thank you so much for what didn't just happen. Wow, that could have been so bad! Oh thank you, thank you, thank you," and "Whew! Yikes. I need a minute to breathe."

The *good stuff* of relationship with God is when you find out your child stole something from another student at school, and you take your fear for your child's future, shame at how this reflects on you as a parent, aching at what your child must be feeling, and/or annoyance at having to deal with the situation (and let's be honest, it's never on a day you have time to!) straight to God along with your earnest request for wisdom in responding.

Taking your emotions to God, walking through the open door, is as simple as talking to him throughout the day, turning to him with every blip on the emotional radar, every stronger eddy in the current of your feelings. Christian author and thinker Paul Miller once quipped that anxiety is wasted prayer.[1] Was Miller saying that any experience of concern that bad things might happen is sinful? No. He simply meant that doing anything with our fears, especially chasing your thoughts on the hamster wheel of anxiety, short-circuits the very purpose for which God gave us the capacity to feel anxious. Our anxieties are meant to lead us straight to him. Every time.

Do not be deceived. There are a thousand false answers to our anxiety. A myriad of other places we take our feelings for comfort. Everything from drug or sexual addictions, workaholism, abusive behaviors, and anorexia to Facebook, snacking, SportsCenter, and even thick theological volumes can divert us from the path our emotions are trying to pave to bring us to our Father. And, by the same token, every tear, sigh, explosive exhalation, grimace, grumble, or guffaw taken directly to the Friend who makes his home in our hearts is a taste of the fellowship we were made for.

So don't keep your feelings to yourself. Don't even identify, examine, evaluate, and act on them by yourself. Instead, take him your heart as often as it wells up within you—no matter what shade the upsurge may be—and pour it out before him. A broken and contrite heart he will not despise, nor will he fail to rejoice with those who rejoice.

Questions for Reflection

As you face your own feelings:

1. What makes it hard for *you* to bring your emotions to God?
2. Stop and talk to God about what you are feeling right now. Even if you aren't "feeling anything at all." The human heart is never, ever empty. Engage with him in this moment by pouring out whatever you find there.
3. How did it go?

---

1. Paul Miller, *A Praying Life: Connecting with God in a Distracting World* (Colorado Springs: NavPress, 2009), 70.

As you help others:

1. Next time you have the chance to pray for someone in person, ask how this person is feeling about his or her situation before you pray, and make sure you pray not just for the situation but also for the feelings your friend describes, especially that God would meet this individual in those emotions.

2. What is hardest for *you* about helping others take their emotions to God?

10

Engaging Relationships

Having established that our emotions play an absolutely vital role in our relationship with God, we turn now to look more closely at the *way* our emotions connect us with God and with others. Scripture gets at this using the image of the body. Paul writes that Christians are "members" of one body (1 Cor. 12:12). Like the parts of a body, we are intimately knit together, and for the body to function well, its parts must be intimately joined to each other. A hand that isn't aware of what the rest of the body is doing and experiencing isn't very useful. If one leg doesn't know what the other leg is doing, the two limbs can't coordinate their movements to move the body forward or keep its balance. So Paul writes that being knit together in love means that we must "rejoice with those who rejoice, weep with those who weep" (Rom. 12:15). When the other person is honored or is experiencing good things, you rejoice with the blessed individual. When he or she is suffering or in sorrow, you feel the pain right along the one afflicted. This is how the body acts and moves in coordination and love.

It sounds pretty straightforward, but it can be pretty difficult and messy. Sometimes emotions seem to be more of a barrier to connection than a help.

Connecting Gone Wrong: Roger and Jean

Consider Roger and Jean. They were in the car and running late—again. Icy silence filled the air. No radio. No conversation. Roger just stared at the road ahead with focused determination. As he jerked the car into the passing lane, accelerated, and sped around the cars ahead, Jean clenched the armrest and pressed a foot into the floorboard as if working an invisible brake pedal.

Suddenly she hollered, "Roger, slow down! You're going to get us killed!" Roger responded with a withering look. "Roger, I'm not kidding! Don't you care if we get killed!? Either slow down or pull over and let me out!"

"Stop being hysterical, I'm not going that fast! You're the reason we're running late in the first place, and I'm not in the mood for your back-seat driving!" he snapped back.

There's plenty of emotion in this conversation but it certainly isn't helping them to connect. Just the opposite. Roger and Jean are intensely aware of their *own* emotions but unable to enter into and understand the experience of the *other*. In a sense, they are two members of a body separated by their emotions.

So, what's going wrong, and where do they go from here?

A Script for Relating

It often serves relationships best when emotions have a clearly defined role to play and we know when it's time for them to do their part. One way to encourage this is to follow an order of procession for emotional connecting—kind of like a wedding ceremony. Each emotion has a purpose, place, and a time to step to the fore. You can think of this order as a script, because it often doesn't feel natural and takes practice. Most people are accustomed to emotions pushing their way to the front of the line in a jumbled, confused mess, or one emotion dominating the others so that efforts at connecting end up exacerbating conflict rather than promoting harmony. By following a script, you can have some idea how each emotion can enrich the relationship rather than becoming ammunition in a conflict. The script follows three stages that may need to be repeated several times in order to really connect:

1. "This is what it was like for me. What was it like for you?"
2. "So this is what is was like for you [summary]? Am I hearing you right?"
3. "How can we do this differently?" (And possibly) "This must change."

Let's dive into how this script can play out practically.

"This Is What It Was Like for Me. What Was It Like for You?"

The first line of the script can be the hardest to say, because anger is often pushing to get to the front of the line. But we all know how badly things often go when we let anger speak first. We tend to make assumptions and launch accusations at the other person, which only lead to defensiveness and a counterattack from the other. Anger doesn't have to be that way, but when we let it push its way to the front of the line, it tends to displace all the other emotions that help us connect initially—compassion, concern, and patience. So rather than leading with anger, slow down enough to connect with your genuine concern for the other person. Then share that concern as an honest and humble disclosure about what was going on inside of you and a sincere concern about what was going on inside of the other party. This first step is essentially an invitation to disclose and connect through your own vulnerability. You are leading the way.

Vulnerability: "This is what it was like for me." When you are working through your emotions with another person, it's important to begin with your own vulnerability. Vulnerability extends an olive branch of charity instead of leading the conversation with accusations. If Roger were to initiate the conversation with vulnerability, he might say something like this to Jean:

When we left the house, I felt like you were angry with me, and I didn't want to be criticized. I wanted you to know I was upset, but I was so angry, I didn't know what to say, and so I just retreated and got quiet. I'm sorry. I don't want there to be icy silence between us. I want to be close to you. Can we talk about it?

He *wouldn't* say: "Jean, I felt like you were acting really annoying. What was it like for you?" That's just an attack thinly camouflaged with the words "felt like."

Vulnerability is important because only people willing to stop attacking and accusing and instead to open their hearts to each other will be able to overcome conflicts and grow closer. However, vulnerability is also very difficult; it feels much safer to hold back and blame each other than for each to take ownership of his or her own part in the conflict (even if that feels like only 1 percent).

Understand that being vulnerable, by definition, is taking a risk. (*Vulnerable* comes from two words meaning "able" and "wound.") For example, if Roger does slow down and speak the vulnerable words you just read above, Jean could easily use Roger's statement against him and say, "Well, if you weren't so childish, then we wouldn't have these arguments." But by being vulnerable, you are taking a major step in steering the conversation away from a blame war. It takes two to keep a war going; when you lead with vulnerability, you are retreating from the battle by acting in humility, putting the good of restored relationship ahead of your own comfort or being "right." Being the first to lay down your weapons and express a real desire to understand and be understood can be a scary thing to do. The willingness to take that risk on behalf of the other person, however, is precisely what makes vulnerability so powerful. You are signaling that it is safe for the other person to do the same. Might that person take that signal as a sign of weakness and choose to attack? Yes, but it embodies the grace that God has shown us in Jesus, and that is powerful. We are learning to follow God in faith. "God's kindness is meant to lead you to repentance" (Rom. 2:4).

Empathy: "What was it like for you?" Remember—emotions are about connection, which means both being known and *knowing*. Your vulnerable disclosure should be followed with a genuine invitation for the other person to do the same and your willingness to empathize.

Listening with an eagerness to understand and care is as important as initiating with vulnerability. In the same way that empathy is essential for loving conflict resolution, it is also an essential element of the gospel. The author of Hebrews gets at this when he writes that Jesus "had to be made like his brothers in every respect, so that he might become . . . merciful" (Heb. 2:17). "For we do not have a high priest who is unable to sympathize with our weaknesses, but one who in every respect has been tempted as we are, yet without sin" (Heb. 4:15).

You might say that empathy is an emotional expression of the incarnation. It's a way of saying, "I want to know what this situation was like for you, rather than just imagining what your situation would be like for me." Understand that God didn't *need* to walk around in our world, but he did anyway. The best kind of love wants to walk around in the other's world, to truly draw near even at the level of the heart. Part of vulnerability is saying in effect, "Let me get in your space so that I can truly understand you in love."

Let's take a different example. Suppose a friend tells you her husband has committed adultery. Instinctively, you imagine what hearing that would be like. Rather than asking her how she feels, you think of the anger you would feel if you were in her shoes. So, in anger you say: "I just couldn't stay married to someone who cheated on me! I would kick him out of the house and change the locks so fast his head would spin!" And maybe that's exactly how your friend feels, but maybe not. Either way, you haven't considered the many other things she might be feeling—grief, fear, shame, and guilt, just to name a few. Unless you ask and are willing to understand, you won't know.

To empathize means to wonder what is it like for *her* to be *her*, given *her* history and the history of *her* marriage, and to have *her* husband betray her. By telling her what it would be like for you, you've simply read yourself onto her situation. You've really invited her into your world rather than visiting hers. Only when she has actually started to share her experience and you have begun listening carefully and compassionately have you begun to enter her world.

Being like Christ in your friendship, or in your conflict, means following this vulnerable invitation and disclosure with a holy curiosity that wants to know and care about the other's experience. Genuinely asking, "What was it like for you?" invites others to share their hearts with you and is the first step in moving toward connecting.

"So This Is What It Was Like for You [summary]? Am I Hearing You Right?"

Part of entering another's world in a Christlike way is speaking from the other party's perspective. You must summarize that world in your words. You've got to credibly understand and articulately express the other person's voice so that he or she *knows* that you know. Again, this is fundamental to Christlike love and reflects Jesus's attitude toward us. Instead of appealing to omniscience, God opened his ear toward us in the flesh so that we would "not have a high priest who is unable to sympathize with our weaknesses" (Heb. 4:15).

Charity: "So this is what it was like for you [summary]?" As basic as it might sound, simply restating the other person's perspective charitably, in the most genuine and accurate way possible, can significantly deescalate the conversation. Further, it reestablishes the very credibility, rapport, trustworthiness, and friendliness that the relationship was hopefully built upon. And charitably stating someone else's perspective (which is very difficult when that person's words indict you) grants the person's viewpoint a dignity that would be missing if you merely caricatured his or her experience in order to make your own point.

But anger attempts to push its way to the front of the line again when you perceive inaccuracies and falsehoods implicit in another's perspective. In this case, it's important to remember that your summary doesn't imply an endorsement of the other person's perspective and doesn't need to include an evaluation. If you feel that it's important to make that distinction clear, then you need to say it in a way that reinforces your care for the person and desire to understand: "If that's how you heard what I said, I completely understand why you said what you did. And I don't want you to feel that way. I'm committed to doing what I can. I *care* that you felt hurt."

Understanding and caring about the other person's experience is not the same as agreeing about it. My perspective is still my perspective, and I still may think I'm correct. But we must get to that place of genuine caring about the other party's experience, even if we don't agree with his or her interpretation.

Humility and patience: "Am I hearing you right?" Verifying your understanding of another's perspective is just as important. If the other person gets the sense that you're listening just to earn the right to vent your own frustrations, then your charitable summary isn't going to be meaningful. Asking, "Am I hearing you right?" is meant to express genuine commitment to that person's dignity and worth. It's meant to communicate, "I care more about what's going on with you than winning a fight." And if others don't think you're getting it right, then you need to ask them to help you understand what's missing and keep listening!

In my (Winston's) experience in the counseling room and in my own life, asking this question is often the difference between suspicious disconnection and building a trusting relationship. When I feel I can trust someone because he is handling my perspective with care, my defenses come down, and I become much more willing to enter *his* world. He is building credibility with me. He's putting capital into our relational bank account. I think, *Since you're willing to see things from my perspective, then maybe I can work to see things from yours.*

Jesus doesn't just have an abstract knowledge of who I am and what I experience. He's actually entered into my experience, and I trust him as my High Priest. He's inhabited my world and my experience, so I'm going to follow him now.

"How Can We Do This Differently?"
(And possibly) "This Must Change"

Courage: "How can we do this differently?" The process begins with vulnerability, your willingness to reveal your heart, and at this point vulnerability comes to the foreground again. But here it might be more helpful to think of it in terms of *courage*. You already know how badly things can go. (That's how this conflict heated up in the first place.) But God's presence and his promise to help give you good reason to believe that you can understand and care about each other better, and to hope that you can actually work together to make things better.

It takes courage to do the work of change rather than emotionally withdrawing or walking away.

Suppose Roger and Jean really hear, understand, care, and connect. Jean hears Roger's frustration over running late and owns her contribution to the problem. Roger hears how his impatience and aggressive driving not only were frustrating to Jean but actually made her afraid and wonder if Roger cares. Both acknowledge their sins, repent, and ask forgiveness. But love requires them to look ahead. How can they make this less likely to happen again? Of course, no matter what they decide, there are no guarantees. In the moment, when emotions are running high, they may well have very similar responses, and the cycle will repeat. It will take courage for them not only to seek the Lord's help and imagine how they might make different choices and respond differently but also to believe that they both will.

Anger: "This must change." Anger is one of the emotions that Scripture most often warns us about. We tend to prefer anger to emotions that make us feel weak or vulnerable. Anger is fast, capable of moving from mild annoyance to flat-out rage in a matter of seconds. It's powerful, it physically charges us, and when there's a lack of self-control, it can destroy relationships. No wonder the Bible issues so many warnings about the dangers of anger.

Anger also plays a starring role in defensiveness. In anger, we often become focused on our sense that we are in the right and the other person is in the wrong, and all of our emotional energy goes to making that point. Jean angrily confronts Roger with her sense that he is driving unsafely and doesn't care about her safety. Roger angrily confronts Jean with his sense that she is overreacting and at fault for their running late. Perhaps his aggressive driving is, itself, an unspoken expression of anger meant to "teach her a lesson." Obviously, two people solely focused on proving themselves right are not likely to enter into, hear, or understand each other. Instead, they fortify themselves against each other's attack, they press on with their own, and the conflict escalates.

But to use anger as energy to double-down in defensiveness is to fundamentally misunderstand what anger *is*. God's wrath is not a doubling down but a *giving people over to their desires* (Rom. 1:24) while maintaining a desire for reconciliation. In other words, I can't and won't intimidate you into loving me. That's fundamentally manipulative and doesn't result in love. But I will let you go your own way, and I'll walk away from sinful and damaging behavior if necessary. There's more to say about anger, but that will come in a later chapter.

Anger does have a role to play and can have a voice, but most often it's wisest to soften its voice with humility and concern and withhold anger if possible. If you do give anger the microphone, it's important to understand the *purpose* of anger. Fundamentally, anger's role is to say, "Hey, that isn't okay!" or "This is really wrong!" Anger gives me the energy and courage to address wrongs. Anger is often voiced first because it often arrives first on the scene—when survival is at stake we need it *immediately.* If a criminal breaks into my house and is endangering loved ones, anger will give me the energy to come out of hiding, call the police, and do what I can to protect them.

Once you've engaged in these first few steps of vulnerability and incarnation, if the other person's response is manipulative or harsh, anger can give you the energy and motivation to say, "It wasn't okay then, and it isn't okay now," and to keep saying no to sinful behavior. Then you can keep talking, or take a time out if needed, or perhaps come back to the conversation when you've both had a chance to pray, seek counsel, and think more about the situation. If the other person is especially menacing or abusive, anger may give you the energy you need to step out of the room or even back away from the relationship. Anger gives you the bravery to stop destructive interactions, and that's a good thing.

Nonverbal Communication

It may be helpful to add a final note on the nonverbal nature of communication. *Most* communication in any given conversation has much more to do with *how* something is said, than with the words themselves. In my experience, tone and facial expressions may be greater sources of misunderstanding and conflict than words. Words can be clarified with explanation, but if tone and facial expressions don't line up with your words, or they even contradict them, then it's going to be difficult to connect.

Regarding nonverbal communication, it's important for you to understand that you are responsible for your tone and your facial expressions. If the other person says, "You sound angry, and you're expressing disgust with your face," it's not helpful to say, "That's not what I intended, and I never said I was angry." The other party is trying hard to piece together your perspective. Two practical points can guide you:

1. Be conscious of and intentional with your tone and face while communicating; perhaps even go out of your way to maintain a peaceable tone and kind face. Watch out for eye rolling, heavy sighs, folded arms, and turning your body away from the other person. When trying to connect, keep an open heart and an open posture—sit down to talk, relax your face, face the other person, and even lean slightly toward him or her. It can be helpful to practice saying what you want to say in front of a mirror when preparing for especially emotional and difficult conversations.

2. Try not to be defensive about comments on your nonverbal gestures. We're often not aware of what we are doing with our faces, posture, or tone of voice. If someone is commenting on it, it's worth exploring and considering what your onlooker sees and hears. Apologize for the confusion, check out your tone and expressions, clarify the meaning of your words, and try again. If the other person is expressing nonverbally something different from what he or she is communicating verbally, gently point it out. Ask for clarification, and emphasize your desire is to understand your conversation partner accurately.

Leading with Vulnerability Means Following Christ

Following Christ requires vulnerability. Give voice to some of the emotions that make you feel weaker. They are better invitations to connect than anger. Learn how to talk about your fear, embarrassment, or sense of hurt. Some common experiences that you may need to voice are "I really feel hurt," "I feel rejected" or "neglected," and "I feel ashamed." When you talk about being hurt, you are often being more honest about how you feel at a deeper level, and you are also more likely to have an audience.

When those whom God loved rejected him, he came and spoke to them in person. When they took advantage of his vulnerability and rejected him again, he responded by moving toward them in mercy rather than rage and defensiveness. And no matter what, he is committed to working things out with his children forever, because he loves them.

For this reason, we engage in relationships best when we follow the incarnational love of Jesus. Our best relational moments—the ones we will look back upon with fondness as turning points and bonding moments with our loved ones—will be the times when we entered difficult emotional conflict by leading with vulnerability and empathy, following through with charity and patience, and letting them all frame the legitimate concerns anger may need to express.

Questions for Reflection

As you face your own feelings:

1. Which piece of the "script" most stands out to you?
2. Is the idea of a "script" for communicating emotions helpful to you? Why or why not?
3. What do you want this chapter to change about the way you communicate your emotions? About the way you listen to others?

As you help others:

1. When have you recently seen unhealthy communication about emotions? What was wrong with it?
2. Can you imagine using the "script" in this chapter to help someone work through emotions in a relationship? How would you have him or her engage it?

11

On Nourishing
Healthy Emotions

By this point it should be obvious that a healthy, godly emotional life doesn't just happen. It takes work, time, and grace. An enormous amount of work, actually—and a *lifetime* of grace. But it's a different kind of work than you might think. In fact, all Christians seeking to live faithfully before the Lord and grow in relationship with him *are* working on their emotions, though most aren't consciously aware of it.

We're going to flesh out this work in this chapter and the next in two very simple ways. First, this chapter focuses on how you can walk out Christian faith in ways that strengthen godly emotions. Then, the next chapter will look at the opposite: dangerous practices to avoid that tend to pull your heart and flesh away from emotional maturity.

Happily, we can nurture godly maturity in our emotional lives without mastering a complex list of spiritual techniques or even consciously paying attention to our emotions. By pouring ourselves into simply knowing, trusting, and deepening our love for Christ, we will, as an inseparable result, develop godly feelings.

Our hearts will grow more and more to love what God loves (which will mean hating what God hates as well).

This chapter, then, has a very simple goal: to lay out six accessible practices that will incubate and nourish a godly health and maturity in your emotions across the entire emotional spectrum. These suggestions are *not* tools for changing your emotions. Rather, they are ways to harness wise, normal, spiritual practices that will grow your love for what God loves and gradually mold your feelings to reflect the emotional life of our Lord.

This, of course, does not mean there are only six ways to nurture good emotions in your life! Far from it. So please take this as a nudge to get you going, a gentle push to start your feet moving a few steps down a long road. Our hope is that reflecting on and walking out any of these steps will make it easier for you to identify other areas that can enrich your heart too.

Read Your Bible

Many of you will have a sinking feeling when you see that our first suggestion is to read your Bible. Not only is this about the least novel suggestion you have heard for the Christian life, but it also could very easily feel like a trite answer to a complex topic. Or, worse, it could actually feel condemning and guilt-inducing, as if we're suggesting that if you would just read your Bible, your emotions would all fall in line.

The reason we start with "read your Bible" is none of these ideas. Instead, we start here because reading the Bible is a perfect example of how you don't have to dream up fancy new methods to mature your emotions. Even this most basic of Christian practices can bear rich fruit in your emotional life.

There are three main ways Bible reading does this.

We find treasured passages. The first and most obvious is that we turn to favorite passages in the midst of strong, troubling emotions—such as anxiety, anger, confusion, bitterness, guilt, and despair—and find help.

For example, I (Alasdair) vividly remember a late evening in early 2010, sitting in a colleague's guest room nervously preparing myself to meet with pastors the next day. The future of the counseling center we were hoping to found hinged on the conversations of the next twenty-four hours, and I strongly suspected at least one of these conversations might be strained. I am not prone to anxiety, but anxiety tugged and clutched at me more intensely that night than I had ever felt before or have felt since.

Knowing that the Bible was a good place to go with my fears, I opened to the Psalms, and God kindly placed Psalm 27 in front of me. It begins: "The LORD is my light and my salvation" (v. 1). This reminded me that my hope needed to be in God—not in our counseling center. The psalm continues,

> Though an army encamp against me,
> my heart shall not fear. (v. 3)

If David did not need to fear literal armies, how much more could I claim refuge! It helped that night to see as well that David needed to remind himself repeatedly of the good reasons he had not to fear. I could almost hear David's heart beating with anxiety as he wrestled his own soul toward trust in the Lord. My eyes clung to the words of the psalm that night like a rock climber to a handhold on a steep cliff. I've been back to Psalm 27 countless times and also taken countless other fearful people there in counseling.

Our hearts are shaped by God's Word. Here is a second way the Bible affects our emotions: its words pull our attention toward God's story and the fact that he is real. Words are powerful. Words that we read and hear shape our perspectives. The effect may be extremely subtle, of course. In fact, most of the time we're entirely unaware that words have made any difference at all. But, for better or worse, words always matter. They reinforce our perspectives or undercut them, focus our attention or distract us, force us to pause or hurry us along. This is not just a possibility or even a strong likelihood. It is inevitable. The words we are exposed to mold our hearts far more than we think.

Which words do you want shaping the way you see and respond to the world?

How do the words of Scripture, in particular, alter your perspective for the better? In a thousand ways. They make you think about the trials and faith of the biblical characters, the similarity of your heart to theirs, and God's faithfulness to them. God's words soak your mind in explicit hopes, promises, comforts, reassurances, commands, reminders, and warnings. They call your attention to who God is, who you are, and how the world works. They engage your emotions directly through humor, lament, dry sarcasm, impassioned entreaty, and euphoric exaltation. They boost you up onto your mental tiptoes to peer through a window in history at God's tender care for a young Moabite woman and her widowed Israelite mother-in-law, a youngest son whom God anoints to kill a giant and become a king, a self-righteous murderer who is knocked on his back and becomes a missionary. Words grab your attention and slip into your subconscious as they sing, preach, teach, and narrate.

Make no mistake: every last word in the Bible bids to change you—to change how you think *and* how you feel about the world around you. This does not mean, however, that reading the genealogy of Jesus in Matthew 1 will somehow magically dispel a panic attack just because it happens to be in the Bible. A lot more people would give their children names like Amminadab or Zerubbabel if it did! It *does* mean that reading your Bible regularly over the years will make you a different person. Choosing to let Scripture's songs, sermons, and stories enter your mind is like choosing to eat a balanced, healthy diet: every cell in your body will be affected by access to good nutrients, mostly in ways you're never aware of. As a result, even reading the genealogy of Jesus helps stabilize your hope in the gospel as you learn to appreciate how God works through families, even families that include such unlikely outsiders as Rahab, Tamar, and Bathsheba, as well as people with major moral failings, like Abraham, Jacob, and David.

We encounter God. Finally, the Bible impacts our emotions because when we encounter God's words, we encounter God himself. To read the living Word of God is to relate to him. In Scripture, God both shares his heart and calls you to respond from yours. Reading Scripture is literally reading a message from God to you. It's not *solely* to you, but when God speaks to his people—and if you are in Christ, you are one of his people—his words are intended to transform your way of life.

One simple, practical way to respond to this relational aspect of Scripture is to write out your response to what you're reading as if you were speaking directly to God. In the margins of your Bible or a notebook, lay out your questions, reactions, concerns, and thought processes in *I* and *you* language. In fact, maybe you should even speak your words to God aloud, like you would if you were talking to anyone else! Our "quiet times" (the phrase many of us use for our prayer and Bible reading) should become "aloud times," since speaking out loud forces our prayers to be less distracted and more personal.

Ultimately, whether you write, speak, or do both, every passage says something about who God is and who you are. Each page of your Bible is inviting you to talk to God. So pick up your pen or open your mouth and start with "Reading this makes me think that you . . ." Finish the sentence with whatever is in your heart and mind. Then start and finish another passage.

In our Bibles, we find God reaching across eons, oceans, languages, and foreign cultures to catch our attention and have a talk. Will you listen? Will you reply? Your emotions will be nourished as you do.

Go Outside

Our second suggestion is to go outside more often. Likely the recommendation to be out in nature needs little defense. Most people know that getting outdoors is good for you. But in an increasingly digital age, it bears repeating: you probably need to get outside more than you currently do. And you don't have to stand in a vast open field to benefit; even a city sidewalk has whistling winds, warm rays of sun, and at least a narrow band of sky.

There is no single reason why stepping out under God's sky is good for your emotions. We admit that ten minutes facing into the breeze or feeling the sun on your face won't radically alter your mood most days. However, as with reading the Bible, it's hard to overstate the value of regularly reminding your body and soul that you live on a larger stage and in a larger story than your messy house or the four walls of your office that surround you hour after hour.

The most important way I (Alasdair) have put this into practice has been taking a walk during my work day—six minutes each way to the stone wall in the woods behind my office, a minute or so to stand, breathe, and watch the sunlight on the forest floor, then six minutes back through the pines and young maple saplings. This little stroll past growing plants and trees and singing birds pulls my mind and senses into contact with God. It reminds me that he is the giver of abundant life and has plans for renewing this world. It also reminds me to relax my tensed shoulders and inhale deeply.

Pastor and author John Piper once said that the reason strip clubs board up their windows is not primarily to stop passersby from unpaid peeks. Instead, it is to stop paying customers from looking *out* and seeing the sky. The owners know that if customers see the heavens, they will be reminded that a vast sky full of stars or clouds hovers above them—and mutely refutes the folly of ascribing worth to a passing, pseudo-pleasure.

"The heavens declare the glory of God" (Ps. 19:1), and we need to listen. So while a daily walk won't kick your depression or cement your contentment, it is one of the most practical things most of us can do to steer our hearts in the right direction.

Cultivate *Good* Negative Emotions

It's telling that the sole example of a book of the Bible named after an emotion is not Joys but Lamentations. As counterintuitive (and countercultural) as it sounds, there are actually ways in which you should feel bad more often and more strongly than you do! We do not mean you should seek out melancholy moods for their own sake. Instead, we're simply suggesting that as Christians we need to pour in time and effort to grow in godly guilt, grief, dismay, and the like because, as we have been saying since chapter 1, far too often we short-circuit God's good purposes for our negative emotions. We crush them, deny them, or escape from them rather than letting them do their good and healthy work of driving us to him.

What does it look like to cultivate healthy negative emotions?

Probably the most important way to nurture uncomfortable emotions in our lives is by learning to lament. A lament is an honest, impassioned expression of sorrow, frustration, or confusion. Lament names a loss or injustice and the impact it has had. It is no accident that lament is the most common kind of psalm. The psalmists knew how badly our world is broken and turned instinctively and earnestly to God.

Psalm 13 is a good illustration of a lament. The author asks the Lord, "How long?" several times. He poignantly expresses feeling forgotten, abandoned, lonely, sorrowful, defeated, humiliated, and in deep despair. He asks God to hear him and see him and, implicitly, to have mercy on him. While he ends with clear hope, it is hope in a rescue that is not yet realized. In short, in the midst of anguish, the psalmist persistently pours out his heart to God. The psalms of lament take very seriously God's promise that he cares for us.

Laments honor God in two ways. They stand with God and grieve the brokenness of the world as he does. God hates sin and suffering and will one day eradicate both. Laments yearn, ache, and call for the coming of that day. This orientation drives our souls to see the world as he does, a beautiful story in desperate need of the happy, heavenly ending that only he can bring.

Laments also trust God with something we care about. My (Alasdair's) dad died in February 2007. I remember someone comforting my siblings and me by saying the pain would "grow easier in time." In response, my then-fifteen-year-old sister said that she didn't want the pain to lessen because this much pain was the only way she could ever imagine feeling about the father she loved so deeply.

I believe she was onto something.

When we love passionately and lose something or someone, our grief is a testament to God's good work in creating the person or treasure we've lost. To stay present with the pain of loss as laments do is, in a strange way, to acknowledge God's goodness in giving the gift in the first place. The biblical pattern is not to shrug losses off and move on. Rather, we are to wail in honest heartache at the wrongness of death and destruction of God's beautiful creatures, especially his fragile children. If you truly love others as Christ calls you to, then you will also truly lament when evil of various kinds befalls them.

Laments, however, are not the only way to engage God faithfully in our negative emotions. Guilt, for example, is a vital emotion to embrace. To experience in your gut that you have done wrong and that your only hope is to turn around and walk in the opposite direction is of enormous value. While guilt can easily misfire and lead to wallowing and ugly self-condemnation, its purpose is to turn us to the One who offers forgiveness. Even those of us who beat ourselves up too much actually need *more*, not less, guilt. The self-flagellation of bad guilt is actually a twisted and disguised arrogance; when I don't measure up to my own standards of how good I should be, I feel awful about myself and punish myself. This pride-in-disguise is itself a sin for which we need to repent! But *good* guilt is freeing. It calls us to stop defending our wrong choices and to weep and repent instead. It helps us feel our need to change and leads us to draw near to God and his mercies. Good guilt leads to gospel repentance and joy.

Perhaps most surprisingly of all, there is even a kind of doubt that can actually be a valuable negative emotion at times. Don't get us wrong; the dangers of doubt are very real. All too often doubt becomes a self-centered faithlessness. That is not what we are encouraging! But there are good doubts. We overhear sanctified, God-engaging doubt in the voices of Habakkuk, Job, the author of Psalm 73, the father of a demon-afflicted boy in Mark 9:14–29, and many others. All express deep confusion about the awful situation around them precisely *because* the speakers trust God's character. They are confounded by the success of evil and ask urgent questions of God when his justice and salvation seem painfully absent. This means we can be faithful and still say to God, "I know you are good and don't delight in evil. . . . So how come the wicked seem to be doing just fine while helpless and vulnerable people—especially those I love—are being destroyed?"

Cultivating such a mind-set doesn't mean searching for reasons to question God's reality or character or decisions. It's actually the exact opposite! Engaging godly doubt means bringing him your questions about the gap between the way he reveals himself to be perfectly good and just, on the one hand, and the way he allows terrible evil to befall people we know he promised to protect, on the other.

The list of *good* negative emotions could go on. We are to cultivate a *fear* of the Lord, a *distrust* of false teaching, and a *hatred* of all that is godless and perverse. Ultimately, our goal is not to feel bad more often but rather to be willing to face, and even step into, the uncomfortable and distasteful parts of this world we live in. Each time we do, we can be sure it will mean feeling distressing emotions if our hearts share God's affections and priorities. To love what he loves will mean to hate what he hates and mourn what he mourns. His call that we grow in love for him and each other necessarily means that we must also grow in our capacity to be pained by what goes wrong for those we love in the world that God so loves.

Build Altars

The altar enters the story of Scripture very early in Genesis, long before God commands the Israelites to build altars to him in the tabernacle. And altars remain a central element of how God's people relate to him throughout the Old Testament.

What is an altar?

An altar is an acknowledgment that something important has happened and needs to be remembered. It serves as a long-term memory aid for who God is and what he had done (e.g., Gen. 28:10–22; Josh. 22:10–34; 1 Sam. 7:12). In this sense, then, an altar is the spiritual equivalent of an expensive souvenir. Think of something precious bought on a family road trip, or a gift brought home to beloved children from your travels, or the candlestick from the restaurant where you had your first date. Souvenirs remind you of that place, that event, and that special person every time your eyes fall on them. For this reason, our most precious souvenirs tend to dwell where we will see them often: on the mantle or on the nightstand. Souvenirs compress a story into a single glance.

Like souvenirs, altars communicate by reminding us of something: the great value and worth of the object of our worship. An altar can be a physical object or it can be any regular practice that reminds us of the value of the object of our worship. We need altars to God. They are reminders of his goodness and refreshing tastes of his kind and personal care for us. Our attention is so easily distracted, and our hearts so quickly forget all that he has done for us. It is no accident that Christ gave us bread and wine, elements we can smell, touch, see, and taste, to remind us over and over of his covenant. We consume them regularly until the day he comes back. We need to be told over and over and over again by all five of our senses that our God is with us.

Every one of us needs to build altars that reorient us to God.

What kind of memorial should we build? Almost any kind imaginable! While we wouldn't use stones and burnt offerings, there are many ways to build altars that will regularly call God's faithfulness to mind. Any physical object or intentionally chosen practice can become, in this sense, an altar.

One young woman I (Alasdair) worked with struggled deeply to believe that God really was a concerned and loving Father who cared deeply about her and her life. We zoomed in on the "pearl of great price" parable, and it became our shorthand for the way all her precious "pearls" in life could be safely entrusted to her heavenly Father. So she started wearing pearl earrings (at least they looked like pearls—I chose not to ask if they were real!). When she wore them, every turn of her head shook the two small, white, spherical altars and offered a gently whispered reminder that she was safe with her Dad.

A young man I counseled found himself overthinking his faith and struggling to find any joy or genuineness in his walk with God. Every event, activity, choice, and recreation dragged with it a pressure to self-analyze. Ironically, my friend's intelligence and theological breadth hampered him from approaching God in a natural relationship. In an effort to break through his overthinking, and because he liked to cook, I tasked him to go to the grocery store, buy himself something both healthy and mouthwatering, and savor it, prefaced only by a simple prayer of "Thank you." My goal was not to make him less precise in his theology or less appreciative of how every moment can connect us to God. My goal was to help him build an altar to God through the act of cooking, through tasting and seeing (and smelling) that the Lord was good in a way that would be unclouded by endless analysis.

I have various altars in my own life as well. A picture of my wife and children on my desk reminds me regularly to thank God for the family he's given. I try to play piano five minutes every day, which regularly reminds me how much beauty can flow from even small ventures in self-discipline. When I drink tea, especially during counseling, I try to force myself to focus on the taste and receive it as an experience of God's delight in giving us good gifts. I need these reminders often.

I could name countless other altars, but I'll mention just one more: the triple-A battery I keep on the chair rail by my desk. This little battery refused to die week after week as it powered the audio recorder of a woman I counseled. She often taped our sessions so she could revisit helpful parts of our conversation later (at least, I hope they were helpful!). The little battery-that-could now silently testifies to me (and to her when I point it out from time to time) that God cares for his hurting children, brings and preserves words of hope through his people, and superintends every detail of our lives for our good.

In summary, build altars in your life from whatever "stones" of God's kindness and care are lying around. Such reminders can scale the walls of our distractions and lead formidable truths to capture our attention and hearts.

Cling to Corporate Worship

Unlike the highly personalized and private altars I just described, church services are public, obvious, and communal. Sunday worship moves our emotions because we are surrounded by other visitors to God's house. In his house, surrounded by members of his family, we are tangibly reminded that we are not alone in this world.

Countless preachers and teachers have called corporate worship an oasis for our parched souls under the beating sun of life. This holds true for our emotions as well. Because it has the power to refresh your wilting worship, a church service has the potential to revive godly emotions as well.

Does this mean that showing up on a Sunday morning guarantees a rich spiritual or emotional experience? Of course not.

Church can be hard for people for a variety of reasons—some personal, some due to weaknesses in the church itself (poor sermons, poor music, etc.). Benefitting spiritually or emotionally from church will be difficult for most of us, at least on occasion.

That said, the formal fellowship of shared Sunday mornings has the potential to shape our emotions for the good in several ways.[1] First, being with others who also place their hope in God's character, plan, and power reinforces in our hearts that we are neither alone nor insane in our faith. This can happen by simply walking into the foyer or the back of the sanctuary, before a word has been sung or preached. (If you are in the persecuted church, gathering in hiding, you may well know the encouragement of seeing even two other Christians slip into your covert meeting place. They, too, are risking their lives just to be with others who love what you hold most dear!) To be with a crowd, even a small one, is to be part of something larger than yourself. On Sunday morning we get a small taste of being part of a great sea of individuals drawn together by a larger purpose that binds us in unity and excites us. You're getting a taste of the celebration to come, a communal rejoicing so vast that no Super Bowl crowd would even be audible next to the cries of victory, praise, and delight that will echo eternally in the wedding hall of the Lamb.

All this and we haven't even started singing yet!

The music of corporate worship can be transformative—which is exactly what many of us need. I know, for many families, Sunday mornings can be overshadowed by the chaos of breakfast and dressing the children, getting them into the car and then out again! On top of that, we're often tired from a long week. Far fewer people arrive at church with eager and quieted

---

1. We have been influenced by James K. A. Smith's perspective on the formative power of corporate worship. For a more in-depth discussion, see Smith, *Desiring the Kingdom: Worship, Worldview, and Cultural Formation* (Grand Rapids, MI: Baker Academic, 2009), or his more popular-level work *You Are What You Love: The Spiritual Power of Habit* (Grand Rapids, MI: Baker, 2016).

spirits, in the right frame of mind for worship, than you might think. But reflect on what happens when we lift up our voices together in song. Our lungs, lips, and larynxes work in harmony to bring resonance, volume, and pitch into the air around us. This sound then reverberates out, each of us physically connected by a shared vibration through the room, through our ears, and through our chests. The melody, harmony, and rhythm draw us into the words we sing. A well-crafted melody or effectively played instrument actually underscores the words for our feelings more than words without music ever could. Further, singing together bridles the pace of our reading as we trot through the theological terrain of a song. We take in the meaning of the lyrics in ways we never could if we were galloping along at the usual skim we've learned to use when reading the Bible on our smartphones. In fact, says author Andy Crouch, "singing may be the one human activity that most perfectly combines heart, mind, soul, and strength. Almost everything else we do requires at least one of these fundamental human faculties. . . . But singing (and maybe only singing) combines them all."[2]

If we wanted to, we could flesh out a significant emotional impact for every single element of church services. In communion, we literally taste and see that the Lord is good; we see and smell, touch, and taste the good news of Christ's body and blood atoning for and sustaining us. In the sermon, we not only learn new things about the character of our Father and his call on our lives; we are also moved. Wise listeners ask not only *What did I learn?* but also *Was I encouraged? Discouraged? Why? How so?*

When God's people gather, we receive a great gift from each other: affirmation of our mutual faith and a revitalization of our all-too-often-flagging love for our Lord and his kingdom. Will you grab hold of these benefits to your emotions?

---

2. Andy Crouch, *The Tech-Wise Family: Everyday Steps for Putting Technology in Its Proper Place* (Grand Rapids, MI: Baker, 2017), 191.

Watch for God on the Move

Lastly, seek out and seize every opportunity to hear about God's work in the lives of others. There is no substitute for good stories of our good God doing good work in the lives of people we know. The Psalms tell these stories constantly when the singer extols God "in the assembly of the righteous," telling "Israel" or "the congregation" of all his wondrous works. Similarly, Paul explains that those who have received "comfort" from God are now equipped to comfort others with the comfort they have received (2 Cor. 1:4). Simply hearing how God has tenderly cared for others can be a great encouragement.

I (Alasdair) have a friend and colleague who instinctively notices and speaks about encouraging fruits of the Spirit he sees in those around him and, with appropriate humility, in himself. I find his awareness of God's Spirit at work immensely refreshing. His ability to notice and name areas of spiritual growth reminds me of how hiking with a nature enthusiast like my father-in-law transforms what to me would just be "trees" into cedar, white pine, and shagbark hickory. God has frequently used my colleague's excited account of some spiritual ripening he's seen that day to refresh my soul when I had begun to slip unconsciously into discouragement.

Noticing how God is moving does not have to be a major undertaking. Just keep an open ear for a young man handling his relationship with his parents more maturely, an accountability partner resisting temptation more effectively, or a child sharing about treating a difficult classmate patiently. Observe your community group and reflect on where they've grown in connecting with and caring for each other. Ask your spouse why he seems in such good spirits. Perhaps most basically, ask *anyone* what the Lord is doing in his or her life! 'Tis grace has brought us safe thus far, and tales of grace in others will help to lead us safely home.

Don't Stop There

The six elements in this chapter are all valuable ways to have good emotional hygiene (a phrase that'll probably never catch on). Nonetheless, they only scratch the surface of what you can do to strengthen the way your emotions reflect God's. Ultimately, any aspect of your daily life, carried out with thoughtfulness and faithfulness to your Maker, will be a blessing to your emotions! Anything that is good for your soul will, by definition, also have some positive impact on your emotional health. So take these six ideas as a jumping-off point and get creative. Fill your life with conscious choices to turn the highs, the lows, and even the mundane moments of your daily life into opportunities for engaging the Lord. He will not fail to grow your love for him and mature your heart and emotions in the process!

Questions for Reflection

As you face your own feelings:

1. Which of these six points stand out to you as most important to work on in your own life?
2. Which do you feel you are already doing well, or at least are working on?
3. What other ideas or areas beyond these six might you add?

As you help others:

1. Which of the six are you most attuned to in the lives of those you serve? Which one are you least attuned to? What is the biggest takeaway you have for your ministry to others?
2. As we've seen, corporate worship is a spring of emotional health. How might this influence the way you encourage those you are ministering to in your church?
3. What patterns in your life might be hindering you from being a source of encouragement and emotional support to those you seek to serve? Who knows (and loves) you well enough that you could ask him or her to help you see your strengths and weaknesses?

12

On Starving Unhealthy Emotions

Emotions would be so much easier if they were like an old western—if you could know the good guys by their white hats and the bad guys by their black hats. It would be simpler if we could just say that anger, anxiety, and depression are *bad emotions*, and happiness, contentment, and affection are *good emotions*. But as we've seen, that's not how emotions work. We can't just put black hats on some feelings and white hats on others. Like it or not, we have to do the work of listening carefully to the messages our emotions communicate and discerning what parts of the messages are true or false and responding wisely.

This is especially difficult when our emotions are running high. Wisdom requires us to think clearly at the very moment our thinking is being powerfully shaped by those very emotions. Important truths that are obvious any other time may feel irrelevant during an emotional swell. The fact that this is hard—experiencing an overwhelming emotion and processing it at the same time—is one of the reasons we are so tempted to take a simplistic approach to our emotions: "Say yes to these emotions, and no to those." But the sooner we accept the difficult task of saying yes and no to the same emotion, the easier it will be to engage our emotions in a balanced way.

In this chapter, we will explore what to say no to and how to say no.

What to Say No To

Since we can't give a blanket rejection of any particular emotion, here are four messages that we can say no to in every emotion.

"I Am My Emotions"

Say no to thinking and acting as if you *are* your emotions. When we talk to people who feel the most overwhelmed by their emotions, they feel as if their emotions represent *who they are*, or their truest selves. But you are more than what you feel. No one can be reduced to what they feel. When emotions are intense, it can seem as if they take up all your interior space. In part, that's because they are physiologically fortified. In other words, your body is working to maintain your emotional state, so your emotions often don't yield easily to thoughts and beliefs that may feel very powerful at other times. But your emotions aren't everything, important as they are.

Psalm 142:3–4 provides some insight into this experience:

My spirit faints within me . . . !
In the path where I walk
     they have hidden a trap for me.
Look to the right and see:
     there is none who takes notice of me;
no refuge remains to me;
     no one cares for my soul.

We can see in David's mind a descent from "my spirit faints" to "no one cares." Of course, David knows that God cares, which is why he is crying out to him, but he is poetically expressing that it doesn't *feel* that way. When we overidentify with our emotions, we begin to distort our perspective on reality.

Emotions become demanding taskmasters when you believe they are the core of who you are. David, whether he feels it or not, recognizes that he cannot stay in this place, which is why he asks the Lord for help in Psalm 142:7:

> Bring me out of prison,
>   that I may give thanks to your name!
> The righteous will surround me,
>   for you will deal bountifully with me.

David doesn't yet *feel* better because he prefaces this entire plea with "I cry to you, O LORD; / I say . . ." (v. 5). David is still weeping. He still feels trapped. His circumstances haven't changed. But he is refusing to allow that emotion to claim his soul. Instead, as we said in chapter 9, David sees his emotions as a chance to engage God. He does not just cry. He cries *to God*. There is a world of difference in these two ways of responding to emotions. One cry is self-talk that may well leave us continuing to feel alone and overwhelmed. The other creates connection to one who cares, reminding us that God is with us even when our emotions are telling us that he isn't.

"I Need to Act Right Now"

Say no to rash actions. Emotions tend to yank us by the collar, pressuring us to act fast. In part, this demand is communicated through our bodies, as we talked about in chapters 2 and 4. The various hormones stimulating our nervous system when we are upset are God-given ways to motivate us to action when we actually need to act. When a car is bearing down on you, emotions save you by screaming, "Jump out of the way!" You don't need to think in that moment; you need to move! Your physiology is designed to ramp up quickly and maintain that emotional state as long as you need it for the sake of survival.

But in our relationships the immediate need usually is to slow down, not to speed up.

In our relationships we should ask, *What does this emotional pressure mean?* The worst moments of my (Winston's) marriage have been rash moments. In my upset I wanted to say something really hurtful to my wife, because it made me feel powerful—*and it worked*, at least for the moment, but it damaged our relationship. Emotions press us to be rash, because they're meant to help us survive in situations that physically threaten us. We don't have immediate control over our physiology, but we do have control over how we choose to respond. We need to learn to say no to that impulse when the situation is not physically life-threatening, because when we are rash in those situations, it usually doesn't end up saving anything.

Even if the message your emotion is giving you is essentially correct, wisdom and love require you to know more than that. Any emotion that insists otherwise will do great harm to you and others.

Interestingly, it's God's very nature to *be slow and deliberate*. Scripture describes God as "slow to anger" (Ps. 145:8). See how different God is from me? We could even say the same thing about joy. A manic sense of feeling good can compel us to make promises we can't fulfill and purchases we can't afford.

Any intense emotion can provoke you to act rashly. One of the prayers for evening worship from the Book of Common Prayer goes like this: "Keep watch, dear Lord, with those who work, or watch, or weep this night, and give your angels charge over those who sleep. Tend the sick, Lord Christ; give rest to the weary, bless the dying, soothe the suffering, pity the afflicted, shield the joyous; and all for your love's sake. *Amen.*"[1]

The request to "shield the joyous" is significant. It puts joy in the category of sickness, weariness, sleepiness, labor, affliction, and death—because joy can be as much of a blinder to God and reality as any other emotion.

---

1. The Episcopal Church, *The Book of Common Prayer and Administration of the Sacraments and Other Rites and Ceremonies of the Church* (New York: Church Publishing, 2007), 124.

The underlying principle is this: engaging your emotions well takes time. Engaging your emotions means not simply indulging them by doing whatever they want right away. It's actually more of a principle about wisdom than about emotions. Wisdom—carefully considering the many things going on in and around me when I'm upset, as well as God's Word—takes time.

> Good sense makes one slow to anger,
>   and it is his glory to overlook an offense. (Prov. 19:11)

Go slow with your emotions, because *wisdom takes time.*
   Psalm 4:4 teaches this principle when David says,

> Be angry, and do not sin;
>   ponder in your own hearts on your beds, and be silent.

David has a lot of opportunities to act rashly in anger and fear. He wants to harm Nabal, but Abigail is wise and rebukes him, and he listens to her (1 Samuel 25). David has the opportunity to kill Saul in a cave, but he resists his soldiers' instinctive urging to do so (1 Samuel 24). David is distressed about his enemies, but rather than act rashly by taking matters into his own hands, he brings these situation and emotions before God in prayer.

Interestingly, Paul draws on Psalm 4 in Ephesians 4 as he counsels the church on how to deal with conflict and anger. He begins by quoting Psalm 4: "Be angry and do not sin; do not let the sun go down on your anger" (Eph. 4:26). He's not saying, "Express your anger before you go to bed" but rather directing us to the mind-set of the psalmist: "I'm angry, and I'm just going to be still for a while, because I don't want to do the wrong thing. I would rather ask God to deal with my enemies than act rashly."

"I Shouldn't Be Feeling This"

Say no to shame and self-condemnation. I think Christians are sometimes especially prone to shame when engaging emotions, because we tend to develop the spiritual reflex of labeling certain emotions or levels of intensity as bad. Then, by repenting as quickly as possible to escape the shame, we don't really understand what's going on in our hearts and miss the opportunity to really grow. Unpleasant emotions simply become witnesses who show up to condemn our hearts.

But we need to say no to the temptation to shut down our emotions before we've really understood what the emotion is communicating. When we feel the need to shut down and escape, including the shame of experiencing them, it's easy to fall prey to dangerous escapes—drugs, alcohol, sexual sins, and a host of others. So, for example, I can acknowledge that my anger is problematic, and I know I'm especially prone to anger around my coworker, but the solution isn't to ignore it. Instead I should slow down and search my heart. *What does this mean? What exactly is making me so angry? What is God trying to show me, and how can he help me?* The anger is undoubtedly telling me very important things. Always examine yourself along these lines:

- What is my emotion telling me about me?
- What is my emotion telling me about God?
- What is my emotion telling me about my neighbor?

Until you begin to answer these questions, you won't know how to respond to your emotion.

We find it helpful to think of emotions as a kind of sixth sense. Think about it. The reason you have more than *one* sense is that each one—taste, smell, sight, hearing, feeling—serves as a check and balance on the others. For instance, you can read the expiration date on the milk carton with your eyes, but you won't really know if the milk has soured until you smell it. Still not sure? Give it a taste.

Your emotions shouldn't operate independently either. So when we say, "Listen to your emotions," we're not saying, "Agree with them." We're saying, "Interpret them." Become emotionally literate. Bring them into contact with your other "senses" and what you know about yourself, God, and others when you aren't emotionally charged. Don't want to leave any communi ative value on the table? Don't waste your emotions! Let them se ve you!

We've had a fair amount of experience counseling people who have experienced relational trauma, and in some cases they become very anxious when they have to say no to someone. Usually there are very good reasons. They've been severely punished for saying no in the past. But they don't just feel anxious; they also are ashamed for feeling anxious. They feel immature, like they are captured in an emotional bubble from childhood.

But is that really a sign of spiritual immaturity or moral failure? Imagine you were walking down the street, and a dog bit you. The next time you walked down the street and saw a dog, there's a very good chance you would feel anxious. Your anxiety would be doing what anxiety is supposed to do by reminding you that dogs can be dangerous and prompting you to ask, *Is this dog safe or not?* Of course, if the anxiety is paralyzing or so severe that it keeps you off the street altogether, then there is more to understand and work to be done, but anxiety itself is not the problem.

If you've been mistreated in relationships, use your anxiety about relationships to slow down, not speed up. Rather than avoid the person who evokes your anxiety, articulate the anxiety to yourself: *I know how people act. I know how much they can hurt. I'm going to move slowly and carefully until I know this person better. Is this person doing something that is signaling danger?* Don't just silence your own anxiety. Make it work for you. For instance, I (Winston) often feel anxious before I speak publicly or deliver a homily, but I don't put myself down for it. I feel anxious because I've learned the hard way that I can really blow it if I'm not well prepared. So when I'm anxious about my homily, I think, *Maybe I should spend more time working on this one. I don't feel like I'm ready just yet.* My anxiety is helping me to be responsible and wise.

"This Is All or Nothing"

Say no to black-and-white or all-or-nothing thinking. Black-and-white thinking always exacerbates and intensifies emotions. Extreme thoughts produce extreme emotions. If I say to myself, *This is awful*, then I will experience "this" as "awful." All-or-nothing beliefs that produce all-or-nothing emotions aren't generally helpful in complex situations or relationships. For example, we can't navigate relationships wisely if we only have the categories of "good people" and "bad people." The messy truth is that even good people sometimes do bad things or unwittingly harm us. And even people who may do many bad things sometimes actually do good things and may even love us.

For instance, if I hold the black-and-white belief that anger is the opposite of love, then when my spouse is angry with me, I'll feel not only that she is angry with me but also that she doesn't love me. It's unpleasant when someone you care about is angry with you, but it's pretty devastating to believe that person doesn't love you at all.

Or try this one: "Good people love their parents." What does it mean that I don't *like* my dad because he is manipulative? When he manipulates me, I not only feel bad; I also feel like I'm a bad *person* to boot, because I must not love him. As we highlighted in chapter 3, while right and wrong, good and evil, and other opposites are very real, for the most part, the world and everyone in it is a mixture of good and bad. God created the world good, but it is fallen, along with everyone it. Therefore, as a mixed person, living in a mixed world, with other mixed people, you may well respond to the complexities of the people and situations around you with complicated and mixed emotions. My spouse isn't *all* good or *all* bad. When I come into contact with the goodness of my spouse, I feel good. When I come into contact with the badness, I feel bad. And sometimes it happens all at once, and I feel more than one thing at a time.

This is why we shouldn't assume our initial experience of our emotions in a given situation is the only one or the correct one.

Romans 12 instructs us: "I say to everyone among you not to think of himself more highly than he ought to think, but to think with sober judgment, each according to the measure of faith that God has assigned" (v. 3).

The Bible instructs us to view the world with sober judgment, recognizing that it is a mixed bag, neither totally bad nor totally good—and to view ourselves and our relationships in the same way. A biblical view of life is this: we live in a good world that's gone bad. All Christians have good going on in them, but they also have ongoing sin.

The Bible tells us that when Ezra had rebuilt the foundation of the temple after Solomon's temple had been destroyed, many young people were overjoyed to have a temple, but many older people wept because it did not match the glory of Solomon's temple. During a feast to celebrate the new foundation, a great shout went up, the young people shouting for joy, and the older ones wailing in sorrow. "People could not distinguish the sound of the joyful shout from the sound of the people's weeping, for the people shouted with a great shout, and the sound was heard far away" (Ezra 3:13). Who was in the right: the people who rejoiced or the people who mourned? They both were right. It was *okay* to feel both.

Instead of developing an *either–or* perspective on the world, develop a *both–and* perspective. There *are* absolutes in God's universe. But our experience is sandwiched by *both–ands*. So reject black-and-white thinking. More often than not, it obscures truth rather than fortifies it.

Do Both

Our emotions will require us to say no sometimes, but we shouldn't put particular emotions in the "no" box as always bad or signs of moral or spiritual failure. You can say no to the things that usually make matters worse without saying no to the important things we need to hear and learn from even the most negative or painful emotions. Saying no to the four errors above is one way of obeying the command "Let not your hearts be troubled" (John 14:1) without developing an unhealthy shame over your emotional life. Do not let your hearts be troubled, *and at the same time,* cry out to the Lord as David does in Psalm 142. Do both. And God in Christ will carry you through an experience that may be impossible for you to understand in the moment.

Questions for Reflection

As you face your own feelings:

1.   When are you most tempted to act rashly? When you are angry? Afraid? Can you think of an example of acting rashly that didn't end well? What can you do to slow yourself down when you are tempted to act too quickly because of how you feel?

2.   Do some emotions especially leave you feeling embarrassed or even ashamed? Can you think of why God has given you those emotions and how they are important?

3.   Think of a time when you had an especially strong and unhelpful emotional response to something. Can you identify any black-and-white thinking at work? What might a more accurate or balanced understanding of the situation be?

As you help others:

1.   Take note of an especially upset or angry person on television or in a movie. Listen to the dialogue and see if you can identify all-or-nothing beliefs that would explain this person's response. Start practicing this kind of observing and listening as you interact with others.

2.   Sometimes when you are interacting with especially upset individuals, there are things you can do to help them slow down rather than escalate and act rashly, such as asking them to sit down with you (rather than pace or stomp around, etc.). What other things might you do to help another person calm down?

PART 3

ENGAGING THE HARDEST EMOTIONS

13

Engaging Fear

If you've stayed with us this far, then you know at least two things about the Bible's view of emotions: they are shaped by what you love, and you should engage them wherever you find them. In this final section we will take the framework we've hammered out in the first two-thirds of the book and apply it to some of the most common troubling emotions. Thus, each of the chapters in part 3 will look at how one particular emotion *communicates*, *relates*, and *motivates* (as we laid out in chap. 2) and then offer suggestions to help you *identify*, *examine*, *evaluate*, and *act* (as we talked about in chap. 8) in response to that emotion.

We begin with the emotion of fear for two simple reasons. First, "fear" comes to us with an incredible number of names in the English language (we haven't done the research but wouldn't be surprised if this were true of most or all languages). Words like *uneasy*, *worried*, *nervous*, *anxious*, *tense*, *uptight*, *spooked*, *haunted*, *scared*, *afraid*, *panicked*, *terrified*, and *petrified* occupy slightly different points on the spectrum, but all express some version of the same core experience. As with the Inuit, who supposedly have more than forty words for different kinds of snow, when your vocabulary balloons with terms for the same core concept, you know you've hit on a profound cultural concern.

The second reason we start with fear is simpler and more personal: you may well have picked up this book because you struggle with fear. How do we know that? Because fear is everywhere. Everyone deals with it, but, unlike anger, which everyone deals with too, fear is much more commonly recognized and admitted. Fear is certainly the most common emotion we've seen drive people to seek counseling.

We are not trying to provide an exhaustive approach for dealing with fear; hundreds of other such books already exist. Our hope is to help you see your fear a little more clearly and deal with it more effectively so that you can profit from and apply the rest of this book as much as possible.

With all this in mind, we will answer two questions: What is fear, and how should we engage it?

What Is Fear?

What Fear Communicates

Fear, whether mild uneasiness or abject terror, has a simple message: something you value is under threat. Something bad might happen to something you care about. The future holds potential for loss.

Because of this and because fear is so common to us, your fears are probably the single best map of what you actually value. Fear points directly to what we treasure, whether health, wealth, acceptance, comfort, straight As, or winning a game of tiddly-winks. You'll be more nervous about having enough money to make mortgage payments than about whether you have a stick of gum because you care more about having a house than about having a nice snack (unless you're sixteen and on a first date and you forgot to brush your teeth). You'll lose more sleep at night worrying about your children than about your chickens.

Communicating value is exactly what Paul's "anxiety" is doing in 2 Corinthians 11:28. As we discussed in chapter 2, Paul is not confessing sin to his readers when he tells them, "There is the daily pressure on me of my anxiety for all the churches." No, he is honestly expressing what is on his heart: the church, God's kingdom, the welfare of his brothers and sisters in Christ. He knows all too well that wolves in sheep's clothing beset the fledging congregations he has hatched. He is rightly concerned over the young faith of those he has brought to Christ, the daily temptations believers face to be selfish and self-indulgent, the danger of internal conflict in the body, and so on.

It speaks extraordinarily well of Paul that his greatest suffering, the capstone at the end of a long list of grueling trials in ministry, is fear for the survival and flourishing of Christ's bride.

To be sure, Paul's anxiety isn't nervous nail-biting. Instead, his letters show fear that is deeply compatible with, even *driven by*, his faith because it flows from his love for God and his spiritual children. It's a fear that leads him straight to God. Of course, most of us are slower than Paul to run to God in our fears, and fewer still can honestly say their deepest concern is the glory of God and the welfare of the church. Fundamentally, however, whether our fears are as godly as Paul's or not, we learn a great deal about our true values and deepest commitments when we look at the constellation of our fears.

Where fear flourishes, there your heart will be also.

How Fear Relates

Our fears not only tell us what we love; they also push us toward extremes in relationships. Fear urges us to either jump back from others or cling to them like driftwood in a shipwreck, depending on our perception of what will most likely make us feel safe.

Take, for example, a woman afraid of being judged by friends at church. One natural strategy would be to pull away from her friends and keep a safe distance so that they see only what she wants them to see. This also leaves fewer touch points where her friends could evaluate (and thus judge) what she does or says. It limits her exposure to the telltale signs of disapproval in their faces, voices, and unspoken choices, for which she is on high alert. Such a strategy can easily become a self-exacerbating cycle. The more she keeps others at arm's length, the more weight rests on each encounter she does have. The added pressure on each encounter in turn increases her sense of anxiety (because the relationship has become more distant and thus fragile). Then, heightened anxiety will likely lead this woman to be more undone by even slight hints of judgment she rightly perceives. It will also make her more likely to read condemnation into words and gestures where it is completely absent. Naturally, all of this will reinforce her sense that she needs to pull away to protect herself, deepening the cycle.

On the flip side, imagine a slightly awkward young man who has experienced repeated rejection from girls he has been interested in but who now is in a dating relationship. He will probably be overattentive to his girlfriend's every twitch or mood, overeager to spend time, overquick to do whatever she wants when they go out. In short, he will cling to her for reassurance about the relationship and for evidence he's still in her good graces. Many women will find such attention pleasant at first, but inevitably it eventually smothers actual love, trust, and attraction. Though our young friend would not put it this way, he values *having* a girlfriend more than the girl herself, and she always eventually feels it.

While these examples show how fear can lead us to unhealthy and self-serving relational patterns on both extremes, fear shared honestly and without manipulative intent can greatly strengthen relationships. Nothing so powerfully quenches the fire of fear as the presence of someone we trust. In fact, even someone we don't know well can bring a surprising amount of comfort.

Counselor and author Ed Welch, our colleague, talks about his sheepish discovery that he felt less nervous taking the trash out at night in the alley next to his house simply because his cat was there with him! How much greater, especially in our fears, is the underappreciated promise of Scripture that God will be with us!

How many times have we heard ourselves casually pray—often throwing in the phrase while thinking what to say next—that God would "be with" someone? The hope and comfort of God's commitment to be present and stand with us, drawing close and never leaving, are terrible things to trivialize. After all, if a friend or even a cat with us takes the edge off our fears, how much more the abiding company of Immanuel?[1]

God chose to come among us in the flesh, enter our hearts with his very Spirit, and ultimately bring us to be physically with him forever. Surely such intimacy is beyond our comprehension. Yet, while this is vastly beyond sufficient for us, God does not expect or even want us to go it alone during our lives on this earth; he actually built us to *need* each other as well. He is enough, and yet he has chosen to use the fellowship we have with each other to encapsulate and reinforce his presence with us. "Where two or three are gathered in my name, there am I among them," Jesus said (Matt. 18:20). Thus, while there are exceptions to every rule, you will be better off in your fears when you vulnerably share them with a trusted friend.

How Fear Motivates

The classic phrase you hear is that fear energizes us toward "fight or flight." This is a helpful summary. To clarify and expand this slightly, fear motivates us to seek *safety*, *control*, and *certainty*. All three are good and right things to seek in the face of danger.

All three, however, can go bad in a hurry.

We've watched countless people—whether a wife feeling hurt by her husband, someone who was grievously sinned against as a child, or simply someone with a timid personality—grasp after safety, control, and certainty *at all costs*.

---

1. *Immanuel* is Hebrew for "God with us" and is the name the prophet Isaiah gives to the Messiah, God come down to bring justice and peace. God's incarnation in the flesh was the most stunning act in history, and the breathtaking nature of his choice to remain with us through the constant, abiding presence of his Spirit, which even David, Moses, and Abraham did not experience, is impossible for us to fully grasp.

But anything pursued at all costs will ultimately cost more than you can afford.

Safety is great, until you cling so tightly to it that you are no longer willing to step out of your zone of (perceived) refuge even to love others or obey God. Good desires for responsibly shaping our environment or obtaining confident clarity about the outcome of our choices easily become ugly demands for a total control and absolute certainty we creatures were never meant to have.

Fundamentally, the problem with all three of these methods of guarding against our broken and dangerous world is that they present a frightfully strong temptation to trust in ourselves rather than God. In Psalm 20, the psalmist says that some "trust in chariots and some in horses" (v. 7), meaning any and every kind of power we muster for ourselves. He contrasts this with a better trust, a trust in "the name of the LORD our God" (v. 7). When safety, control, or certainty becomes our fundamental hope in the face of fear, we are trusting in chariots and horses—which is to say, ourselves. Why do we lean on our own strength? Because at least we know what we are getting (or so we think). Yet, in our desire to be safe through maintaining control and certainty, we implicitly accuse God of not having our best interest at heart. Such faithlessness in God's good plans for us and our safety have been at the heart of sin since Adam and Eve in the garden of Eden.

We'll say it once more: safety, control, and certainty are not bad! Proverbs urges us to seek safety, saying the wise see trouble coming and hide themselves (22:3). And Scripture constantly calls us to seek wisdom and to see truth clearly, which is a kind of certainty. The Bible even has an extremely high view of control, if by "control" you mean the right exercise of whatever strength and responsibility you have. Whether you are a business executive organizing deals or a three-year-old organizing dolls, bringing order and fruitfulness to your world is good. Indeed, Paul spills a great deal of ink calling church leaders to direct and shape the growth of their congregations' faith and community. In short, the problem is not with self-protection or the desire to bring order and predictability to the world around us.

Instead, the caution we want to give is simply this: in this fractured life, you will never be completely safe, fully in control, or 100 percent certain of what is coming next. You were never meant to be. Instead, dangers, dependence, and uncertainties are signposts that point us not to a strategy but to a Person: the One whose control and utterly certain character are our only real safety.

Don't trust your life and treasures to your mind, your bank account, your personality, or your accomplishments. They are all chariots and horses that can't save (we've not met many people who struggle with putting their trust in literal chariots these days). Your only path to real safety lies in trusting God by engaging him in your fears.

How Should We Engage Fear?

Identifying Fear

As is true for any emotion, engaging fear starts by simply realizing it is there. Here are some typical fingerprints that fear leaves.

Physically, strong fear tends to cause shortness of breath, increased heart rate, clammy palms, tensed muscles, and racing thoughts. Nervous twitches (in the face or a constant fidgeting of hands or legs) are not uncommon too. Milder, more baseline fear might show up as digestive issues (ulcers and irritable bowel syndrome can both result from long-term anxiety), headaches, fatigue, and, frustratingly, a whole host of other difficult-to-pin-down symptoms. Basically, given enough time, fear can gnaw on pretty much any part of your body. This doesn't mean that every unexplained physical symptom stems from unaddressed anxiety! It does mean, however, that your fears are probably having a bigger impact on your body than you realize.

Fear also drives us toward patterns of behavior. Some find themselves checking things repeatedly to make sure they are okay, even when they know what they're going to find (a condition known as obsessive-compulsive disorder in its more intense forms). Others expose their fear by giving constant warnings to those around them to be careful, not climb so high in the tree, not take that risk, and so on.

Perhaps the simplest telltale sign of fear in your life is a tendency to ask *what if* questions: What if we don't have enough money to cover this or that? What if we get there and they've already left? What if no one likes my project? What if I'm not ready when they call on me? *What ifs* look to the future and import all the angst of possible dooms while writing the presence and help of God out of the picture.

Lastly, given that fear communicates what is important to you, there's a good chance you are feeling fearful if something or someone you care about is under some kind of threat, even if you aren't aware of feeling anything at all. For example, you may be aware that your child is being influenced by a bad crowd or that your job might be eliminated without being aware that you are anxious. It stands to reason, however, that if someone or something that matters to you (including yourself!) is in trouble or has an uncertain future, fear is probably lurking close by.

Examining Fear

Now that you've identified some form of fear in yourself, it's time to look at what is going on in that fear. Our examination will hunt especially hard for traces of two things: what you are caring about and what you are actively doing (or not doing) to deal with the fear. Here are three helpful questions to get you started.

In what contexts do I feel this fear? This first question is asking what factors are pressing your fear's buttons. Is there a particular location that makes you nervous every time you're there? For example, some people are afraid to go home, because of tension, physical violence, or loneliness. Others become anxious in the dark (a fear far more common among adults than you'd think!).

Some people fear a particular stretch of road after an accident. People fear churches, elevators, airports, forests, or driving in a city. I (Alasdair) get spooked when swimming in water if I don't know how deep it is.

Another kind of context is time. Certain seasons, events, or times of day can produce anxiety. Some people, for example, dread the holidays, painful dates on the calendar associated with grief, or dates with high expectations (Valentine's Day is often more stressful than romantic).

Still other fears swirl around people and activities. Are there particular people in whose presence you immediately tense up? What about particular activities—prepping dinner, driving across bridges, using public restrooms, touching door handles, playing sports, presenting at a meeting?

A wise examination of your fear starts by observing whatever is happening around you when you feel afraid.

What are you doing about your fear? The second question follows on the heels of the first. What do you find yourself doing in response to the places, people, times, or activities that spark your fear?

Do you self-medicate, or escape with alcohol, Facebook, mindless smartphone games, daydreams and fantasies, or overwork? Do you plunge deeper into the swirl of your anxious thoughts, racing endlessly to solve problems in your head, like a hamster on a wheel? Do you get irritable and critical of those around you? Do you turn honestly and desperately to prayer?

Remember though: the fact that you may not be proud of your reaction doesn't mean the underlying concern itself is invalid! We'll say more about this in a moment, when we talk about how to evaluate your fear.

What are you valuing? The simplest form of this question is *Why would I care if X happened?* Listen to your fears. They are telling you something very important about the shape of your hopes, your dreams, and, most fundamentally, your worship. Examining your fear is a chance to put names on your treasures, to listen to what they are communicating.

Evaluating Fear

As we've said, fear can be good. Many fears are rooted in valid concerns for valid loves. Think of Paul's care for the churches, leading to his anxiety in 2 Corinthians 11:28; his love for the Philippians, producing anxious concern to let them know one of their number had recovered from illness (Phil. 2:25–29); his familial relationship with the Thessalonians, compelling him to send Timothy to find out if their faith and fellowship were holding after he left (1 Thess. 3:5).

On the other hand, our daily experience and the story of Scripture are full of examples of fear shuttling hearts away from God rather than herding them toward him.

It is easiest to start by evaluating your reaction to your fear rather than the fear itself. Ask, *Is my reaction to this fear godly and constructive, or am I acting in destructive and sinful ways?* Now remember, as we just said above, a poor response does not necessarily mean the fear you are responding to is wrong or coming out of a disordered love. That said, if your fear is encouraging isolation, anger, self-medicating, health issues, growing distance between you and the Lord, or things like these, *something* is out of place. Your prayer in such moments is that God would help you see what is wrong, whether that is loving the wrong thing, loving the right thing too much, demanding certainty and control to protect something you rightly love, destroying more important things in an effort to save whatever you fear is at risk, or some other faulty response. The Bible offers us a reorienting hope in our fears: no matter what the danger or what we are valuing, God can be trusted with our treasures, and every fear ought to drive us straight toward the Lord in prayer, obedience, and fellowship!

A second, slightly harder evaluation question follows: *How likely will the feared event come to pass?* Fear is a notorious exaggerator and false prophet of doom.[2] While fear rarely evaporates simply because you realize the chances of harm are low, evaluating the magnitude of the threat is still important in preparing to respond. Many of us have had that itch in the back of our minds that we forgot to lock a door at home after we left, even though we know we probably did it on autopilot. While it would be a big deal if the house were broken into, realistically the chances are extremely low that we forgot; and, even if we did, there is a good chance no one would take advantage. The point is that evaluating fears as overblown can be rightly relieving.

On the other hand, as I (Alasdair) write these words, Hurricane Irma is howling across the Atlantic Ocean toward Florida with a projected landfall in the next forty-eight hours. Hundreds of thousands of people along the coast, in low lying areas, and in trailer parks have been ordered to evacuate. These people don't know for sure what will happen, but their fear of the storm destroying their homes and killing them if they stay is definitely justified by the high probability that their communities will be leveled by a storm surge. Here is an example of fear rightly warning people of a very realistic danger, and our evaluation ought to take that into account.

So what if, as is very often the case, you're not sure how likely the fear really is? What if you suspect you're being overdramatic, but you don't feel able to trust your own judgment or evaluation?

Ask someone you trust about it!

A closely related issue needs evaluation as well: how big a deal would it be if your fear came true? Say, for example, you've lost a receipt for the new toaster you bought. The chances of needing to return the toaster under the warranty may be quite small, but there *is* still a chance. However, even if it does break and you can't get a refund because you lost the receipt, your loss is small. It's just not that big a deal if you end up having to buy a new toaster

2. Edward T. Welch, *Running Scared: Fear, Worry, and the God of Rest* (Greensboro, NC: New Growth, 2007), 51–52.

or go without bagels and English muffins. Sometimes, however, our fears fixate on the lost receipts in our life, and we worry a lot about fairly minor trials that would have a minimal impact even if the worst-case scenario came to pass.

The previous two evaluation questions—important as they are in seeing our situation clearly and even bringing a certain amount of relief—do little to help us bring the core of our fears to the heart of our faith. Here then are two final questions that probe deeper and pave the way for the gospel to meet us, whether our fears hit us or pass us by.

First, *should* you even care about this threatened thing in your life? Or, to put the question a different way, how does God see your situation? For example, a man might be deeply afraid that his cherished secret life with pornography will be discovered. In this case, the point is not whether his fear is highly realistic (his wife is going to see the credit card report) or extremely unlikely (he's a tech guru who covers his tracks meticulously). The point is that he should not be treasuring this awful cancer in his life in the first place. Instead he ought to actually *long* to be found out. In fact, he ought to bring himself into the light and confess his sin to his wife and close friends. Now, all of us can and should have compassion on him even as he dreads the shame of his sin being exposed; all of us have sinned in ugly ways, and it does indeed hurt when others see how dark our hearts can be. However, the fear of losing his beloved digital mistresses is fundamentally flowing out of a love for something he ought to hate. He badly needs to evaluate the heart of his fear and see that the problem is the object of his love, not the extent of his anxiety.

Second, even if you *should* value the thing you fear to lose, has healthy valuing become poisonous idolatry? Sometimes it isn't pornography but a successful ministry or a sunny day for your cookout. Ministry and sunshine are good desires. But either can ascend to the throne of our hearts and become a cruel tyrant rather than a gift from God we hope for but don't depend on. Fear exposes the idols of our hearts very effectively, just as it also puts a spotlight on the good places where God has shaped our desires in righteous and healthy ways. Thus fear gives a vital message to the popular pastor who dreads going to the pulpit Sunday mornings because each new sermon bears the mounting weight of sustaining his reputation: the godly goal of a flourishing ministry is warring against God himself for his heart.

What is your fear telling you about what *you* love?

Acting in Response to Fear

What then should you do about your fear?

It depends.

It depends on what your examination and evaluation show you. It depends on how important or troubling a pattern you are observing. It depends on what else is going on in your life. We can make a few general suggestions, however.

First, and foremost, learn to turn to Scripture. We've mentioned how Psalm 27 speaks to our anxieties. Even a literal host of heavily armed men trying to slash and stab you cannot overcome the "stronghold of [your] life" and his protection, in this life and the next. First Peter 5:7 is stunningly simple: hurl your fears straight into his hands; lay your fragile treasures in his lap; give him your anxiety. Why? Because he cares for you. He "cares" in both senses: he thinks about you, feels for you, has an interest in how you are doing; and he looks out for you, acts on your behalf, takes care of you. He promises to be with his children no matter what, till the end of time and beyond (Josh. 1:9; Matt. 28:20). He promises that he will always see your obedience, and not even a cup of cold water given out of love for Christ can be wasted (Matt. 10:42). He invites you to come to him when you are exhausted and overwhelmed (Matt. 11:28–30). He forgives your sins (Ex. 34:6–7a).

This is not a list of abstract truths to memorize (though memorizing them might be very wise!). These are real words from a real God who really can and will do everything he promises. These commitments from a Person you can trust with your very life is an unparalleled reason for hope in the face of fear.

On the other end of the spectrum, it probably doesn't hurt to get your breathing under control. Anxiety may be your heart's way of communicating that your treasure is under threat, but, as we said in chapter 4, it writes that message on the slate of your body. Taking deep, measured, slow breaths and exhaling slowly is a common-sense way to preach the truth of safety in Christ to a body quivering with dread.

Some exercise wouldn't be a bad idea either. Someone once quipped that "exercise is the most underused antianxiety medication." Going for a run rarely makes your fears go away, but just as taking a deep breath or two exerts a check on a pounding heart, so regular physical exertion can reduce anxiety's ability to commandeer your body's systems and convert them into a megaphone for a story of doom.

Ironically, many anxious people struggle to rest as well. Busyness, be it work or play, can drown out the "eternal inner murmur"[3] that things aren't going to be okay. For those who build endless moats of activities to keep fear at bay, rest can feel like putting down the drawbridge and welcoming the invader into the castle keep. It is hard to rest when everything inside you cries out that a successful career, a growing bank account, well rounded children, a flourishing women's Bible study, or a satisfying leisure schedule, any of which take effort from you, is *the* thing keeping you safe! Anxiety pushes many onto a treadmill that never slows down.

If this is you, however, you can't afford *not* to slow down. For you, slowing down is faith.

When you stop checking email in the evening, step down from a leadership role, or even take five minutes to breathe or go for

---

3. Judith Shulevitz, "Bring Back the Sabbath," *New York Times*, March 2, 2003; an online version may be accessed at https://www.nytimes.com/2003/02/magazine/bring-back-the-sabbath.html.

a walk, you implicitly entrust yourself and the things you care about into God's hands. By choosing to rest rather than throw yourself into the fray, you are literally, actively placing the battle and its outcome in God's hands. This doesn't mean self-indulgence or laziness is a virtue. It does mean that refusing to run endlessly and choosing to rest, even in the smallest ways, are a profound declaration that your hope is in God rather than yourself.

On the flip side, many anxious people struggle with procrastination, which is just as fear driven as workaholism. The procrastinator fears the discomfort of doing the work, the uncertainty of the outcome, or both. When you find yourself instinctively punting the most important projects in order to rearrange the sock drawer or play one more game (or read one more paragraph or send one more text or . . .), your need is exactly the same as the anxious worker bee above: to entrust yourself and your work to God. It's just that the application is the opposite. For you, faith will be pressing into what you are responsible to do. In doing so, you entrust the pain of the process (usually overblown in your mind anyway) and the eventual success or failure of your project into his hands (where it has been from the beginning).

What if you find that you somehow struggle with both a faithless self-protective activity *and* a faithless self-protective procrastination? Welcome to the club. What a blessing that our patient Father knows that our fear is quite capable of driving us in opposing directions at the same time. He walks patiently by our side, rescuing us from one danger at a time, teaching us to trust him in our work and in our rest.

Two final types of action apply to us all.

First, seek out and seize opportunities to face your fears. "Face your fears" is, of course, an overused cliché. Yet this is so for a reason: there is enormous value in turning toward, rather than fleeing from, the things we dread. This turning must *not* be an exercise in *self*-trust. But when we *engage* our fears with God, we can have enormous confidence that God will strengthen and grow us. So drive across that bridge. Be honest with your friend about that challenge in your relationship. Keep silent about your irritation rather than harping on it yet again in your effort to control the other person. Go skydiving. Give more money to your church and charities. Take a vacation. Take on a new way to serve.

Second, go on the offensive against any area in your life where you are self-medicating. Resist, cut back, give it up. It's amazing what you learn about yourself when you get rid of a crutch you've been leaning on. (Isaiah records how even God's enemies can see that such weak and ineffective crutches are sharp sticks that pierce your hand when you put your weight on them—Isa. 36:6.) Every time you run to a bottle, a screen, or an event instead of your heavenly Father, you are *dis*engaging from your emotions and from him.

Don't be deceived. Each of the many above actions is ultimately more than an action. Actions always reveal our core beliefs and confidence. We always ultimately vote with our feet. You can choose to make any of the changes in this chapter by simply saying, "Okay, I'll try it." But you won't sustain any change in your life unless the love of your heart changes along with your actions. Only those who are growing in their love for God will be able to trust him. Yet, far from narrowing to a few elites the field of those who can overcome fear, this actually gives hope that all of us can do it! Why? Because every fear brought to the Lord, every anxiety or terror weathered under the shelter of his wings, reinforces our choice to trust. This means that even the smallest acts of faith, in God's mercy, are self-perpetuating. As the Psalms demonstrate over and over, every little taste of God's help and closeness in the face of our fears sparks greater love for God, which he in turn lovingly cultivates into deeper faith and changed lives.

Questions for Reflection

As you deal with your own fear:

1. What have you learned about fear that was new to you?
2. What have you learned about your own fear?

3. Which of the steps (i.e., identify, examine, evaluate, act) is the hardest for you with your fear?

As you help others with fear:

1. Are you good at recognizing when others are fearful? Can you see fear when it is tucked under anger or hidden by self-confidence?
2. What is your instinctive approach to those who fear? To validate them? To challenge them? To comfort them? To run from them?
3. What passages most speak to *you* in your fear? How could you share those passages with someone else? Can you talk about how the Lord has helped you without stealing the conversation and making it about you?

14

Engaging Anger

If fear is the most common emotional struggle Scripture deals with, anger is the most dangerous. Because anger can harness such enormous energy, it has the capacity to vastly reduce the darkness of our broken world by righting wrongs and protecting the myriad fragile good things around us. But it can wreak vast destruction. For this reason, few missions are as worthy as dealing with your anger in a godly way, both when that mission is to curtail sinful rage and when it is to unleash a righteous, redemptive assault on the corrupting power of evil.

Here is the catch: anger wants results fast. If you struggle with anger, you'll find it hard to slow down and listen to this chapter.

So let us make a request of you: don't rush through this material on anger. Don't assume you're not an angry person. Don't read what we've written and say, "Oh, I know who needs to hear this." Instead, read this chapter more slowly than you've read any other, and start with the assumption that your anger is a bigger problem in your life than you think. You may be surprised at what you find. Even if you aren't surprised, however, it would be hard for anyone to think too carefully about or go too slowly in studying the problem of anger in his or her own heart.

What Is Anger?

What Anger Communicates

Anger says, "That is wrong." It is a fundamentally *moral* emotion. In fact, you could say it is *the* moral emotion. When you are angry, what is happening inside is this: your heart is observing the scene before you and crying out that something you love is being treated unjustly. Anger always passes judgment (and judgments, unlike a judgmental spirit, can be right as well as wrong).

Contrary to the fervent contemporary belief of our culture that calling someone else's actions wrong is the worst of sins, moral judgment and righteous anger against evil are actually essential aspects of love. This is why Paul urges us not only to "hold fast to what is good," but also to "abhor what is evil" (Rom. 12:9). The Holocaust was not a different perspective on the value of Jewish life; it was despicable, satanic wickedness. Child abuse, murder, and sex trafficking are not alternative ways of approaching life; they are hell seeping through into our world.

Anger is right to say that some things are terribly wrong.

Yet such anger, like all emotions, flows from love.

This is why there is such a thing as good anger. While it is counterintuitive to most of us, the Bible actually presents God himself as the angriest character in all of Scripture. Yet he is the angriest precisely *because* he is also the most loving character in all Scripture. Remember where we started the book: Jesus standing with tears of anger and grief running down his face as he sees the hideous way death rends the fabric of his Father's creation.

To love deeply is to be deeply angry when your loved ones are victims of injustice.

Many famous voices in the past century—C. S. Lewis, Mahatma Gandhi, Dietrich Bonhoeffer, and G. K. Chesterton, to name a few—have proclaimed the inseparability of love and hate. The opposite of love, they tell us, is not hate but apathy. As English philosopher Edmund Burke is often quoted to have said, "All that is necessary for the triumph of evil is that good men do nothing."[1]

Anger at its best communicates protective love for what God loves. Because it delights deeply in the relationships, people, structures of justice, beauties of creation, and material blessings that God has given, it targets anything that would divide us from God or one another and anything that would destroy what is right, lovely, and fruitful.

At its worst, anger conveys unadulterated self-interest and issues an ultimatum: obey *my* law and *my* will or suffer my wrath. Sinful anger still seizes the moral high ground, but it is a high ground manufactured by my own sovereign preferences. Or, when sinful anger is indeed going after some real injustice, it does so because *I* don't like it and *I* will feel better when vengeance has been done. Make no mistake, the pull of anger is strong. Anger offers the intoxicating experience of playing God—of being lawgiver, judge, and jury and ordering the world according to what *I* like.

Ugly anger is utterly arrogant.

The Devil's great hope is that we will, as Darth Vader urges Luke in *Return of the Jedi*, give in to our anger. Thankfully, God's great gift is the transforming work of his Spirit. He kindly changes our very hearts so that we grow in love for him and for our neighbor in ways that allow love-driven anger to bear redemptive fruit.

How Anger Relates

If you've ever had someone get angry on your behalf when you have been harmed or treated unfairly, you know that it is incredibly comforting. When a friend gets worked up because you've been gossiped about, been unfairly overlooked at work, or had your children get short shrift from a teacher at school, you can't help but feel validated and encouraged. Now, this can turn sour in a second if we recruit armies of sympathizers who reinforce

---

1. Burke said something like this, but researchers have been unable to confirm this wording from his writings.

self-pity in our hearts. Yet the instinctiveness of our desire to pull others into our own pity party reinforces the point: it feels really good to have an angry advocate. From International Justice Mission (a nonprofit rescuing sex-trafficked persons around the world) to a big brother standing up for a younger sibling who is being bullied at school, anger defends those it cares about.

There is, however, a grave difference between a love-filled person who gets angry at a particular injustice and a person who is simply angry all the time. While there is indeed much to be angry about in our world, anger should not perpetually dominate your emotional landscape. No one can live near a bonfire that never goes out without getting burned.

Angry people tend to be highly tuned to the failings of others and are quick to offer or enact correction. Whether through a timid anger offering subtle criticisms—commonly called "passive-aggressive"—or a more brazen approach that raises its voice and bangs on the table, angry people constantly send an implicit (sometime even explicit) message to those around them: don't cross my will or you'll face the consequences. Anger's instinct is to punish and attack whatever (or whomever) it perceives as wrong. It is what makes angry people unpleasant to be around.

To make matters worse, angry people almost never know they are angry people. This makes sense if you think about it: anger says, "I'm right and you're wrong." When you feel deeply right, it is extremely difficult to step back and say, "Maybe *I* am the problem here." Knowing this about us, Jesus gives us one of his most famous instructions: take the log out of your own eye (i.e., deal with your own faults) before you take the speck out of your neighbor's eye (i.e., point out a failing in your neighbor).

People who are angry struggle greatly to perceive their own flaws.

As a result, those who live in a regular state of anger, feeling morally superior and punishing those who disagree, end up driving people away till the angry person stands alone at the center of a relational circle of scorched earth. People feel nervous in the presence of anger, pulling back for fear of critique, judgment, and attack. This in turn irritates the angry person, who feels abandoned and unfairly judged (how dare they treat me as the problem when I am right and have to put up with their junk!), which only makes acquaintances pull back all the more, and the cycle deepens.

How Anger Motivates

Anger seeks justice. Specifically, it protects what it loves, punishes any who harm its beloved, and seeks to reverse the damage. Each of these can bring peace and restoration. Each can also gouge rents in the fabric of creation. The fundamental question in our anger is this: Is our anger constructively serving God's merciful and redemptive purposes, or is it destructively serving our own selfish agenda?[2]

Anger is never content to sit idle. When self-control and wisdom restrain it, they do so with great difficulty. When anger can't find an outlet—perhaps the one who has harmed you is dead now, or you feel that no one would believe you if you spoke up, or you'd lose face if you made an issue of the offense—that anger naturally ferments into bitterness, depression, or shame. (Thankfully this is not inevitable if we engage our anger vigorously with the Lord!)

We have all seen anger in action. It motivates a young child to scream at or hit another child over a stolen toy. It urges your tongue or even your fists to shut others up or cut them down if they disrespect you. It also presses you to prosecute a thief who broke into your home. It fuels your pleas and efforts to break through the self-destructive fog of an addict.

Anger, more than any other emotion, demands to be satisfied with action.

---

2. For an in-depth discussion of the constructive potential of godly anger, see David Powlison, *Good and Angry: Redeeming Anger, Irritation, Complaining, and Bitterness* (Greensboro, NC: New Growth, 2016).

How to Engage Anger

Identifying Anger

Given that anger demands action in response to your judgment that someone has committed a moral offense, we expect to find anger anywhere we find someone in attack mode.

Physically, this usually looks like quickened breathing, flushed face, tensed muscles (perhaps even balled fists). When you are angry, your body feels tight. Long term, anger's seeds sprout up into nearly as many symptoms as spring from fear: hypertension, digestive issues, and high blood pressure, just to name a few.

Now please remember that all these experiences hold true for righteous anger as well, even potential long-term physical damage! Jesus's face surely turned redder as he upended tables in the temple courts, and I have no doubt that staff workers for International Justice Mission risk frequent sleep loss over the atrocities they witness.

Our bodies will and should tauten when we confront evil.

That said, anger is rarely righteous, and most of what you identify will be ugly. If you catch normal sinful anger red-handed, you'll hear a raised voice and harsh, critical words. You might see broken items that have been thrown or smashed (dishes, walls, and phones are especially common prey). Sadly, anger can even delude us into justifying a physical attack on another human being. Bruises and broken bones are the calling cards of an anger problem that has festered and become something severe and urgent.

If you zoom out from the angry person and pan toward the person on whom his displeasure rests, you will find tears, tense silence, anxious placating, or angry return fire. Habitual anger leaves strained or broken relationships in its wake; friends and family are offended or hurt and often tiptoe around the angry person. Distrust surrounds anyone given to anger; where people are hesitant and guarded, you are probably not far from an angry person.

The angry individual herself or himself, however, will see the world quite differently. Anger feels so right, so noble. Thus, while the people in the angry person's life pull back from scorching heat that intimidates them, the person they retreat from feels like a martyr. The angry person's world is full of "idiots," "jerks," and "selfish people who don't play fair." This dynamic is almost humorous when your kindergartener comes to you in a huff because her siblings both want to watch a show (which until yesterday she too loved) that she doesn't want to watch (imagine their audacity!), and she tells you they are "just watching it because they don't want me to get what I want." But it becomes a vile foretaste of hell when a middle-aged man justifies his physical, sexual, and relational abuse because his wife isn't "doing what the Bible says she ought to."

If you find that you always seem to be surrounded by fools everywhere you go, beware. You may be blindly stumbling down the slope toward a serious problem with anger.

One last thought about identifying anger. We have heard people countless times say something like "I'm not angry; I'm just frustrated." Or "irritated." Or "annoyed." While common English usage does indeed reserve the word *anger* for more intense situations than words like *frustrated* connote, do not be deceived: frustration, irritation, and annoyance *are* anger. They just haven't fully blossomed yet. So do not draw a line in your mind between frustration and anger! Frustration *is* anger, and it inevitably becomes anger that rightly bears the name if left unchecked. People tend to make the distinction because it is socially acceptable, most of the time, to be frustrated. You are much less likely to get away with admitting you're angry. It is good, however, to confess, at least to yourself, that your frustration is really anger in its adolescence. Then you can engage the Lord in earnest before the dragon matures, spreads its wings, and begins to breathe fire out into your world.

Examining Anger

The first question to ask is *Why am I angry?* While this is designed to help you *begin* to deal with your anger, we've been encouraged at how simply examining the source of one's anger by saying, "I'm angry because . . ." can itself defuse wrath. Often when we realize the petty source of our anger, the fire of judgment inside begins to sputter and die down. I (Alasdair) remember one particular man who was seeing me for court-mandated anger counseling who said it was life-changing simply to say, "I'm mad because that coffee lid didn't fit and I burned my hand."

What wrong am I perceiving? is another way of asking the same question. Asking the question this way helps you put words on the sense of injustice you feel. As with every emotion, your anger connects to something you care about (at least in this moment). If you are having trouble putting words on the injustice you feel, look at whatever you are attacking (or wanting to attack). Whatever you want to lash out against is either the thing you are angry at or is very close to it (e.g., when you punch a wall, it's not the wall you are angry at, but you probably do so within thirty seconds of an interaction that roused your wrath).

Another helpful question is this: *What is the outcome of my anger?* Is my world or the world of those I care about getting better as a result of my being angry, or is my wrath hurting me and others?

It's important when examining your anger to keep in mind that anger often hides. Escapist patterns—alcohol and drugs, of course, but any method of checking out can serve—can cover a simmering rage. Even simple niceness can mask anger; those too timid to unleash the fire within can be stoking the flames every time they smile and pretend to be fine. Many are unaware that they are angry till they explode. This doesn't mean every nice person—or every addict, for that matter—has a huge anger problem. It does mean that the absence of obvious signs does not mean the absence of anger.

In short, your job in examining your anger is to figure out what kind of judgment you are passing. Once you know what you're mad at and why, you can then begin to discern how valid your anger is and begin to think redemptively about how to handle it.

Evaluating Anger

If anger boils down to moral judgment (it does), then the first key matter on which to evaluate your anger is this: Is your moral judgment in this situation valid? Or, put another way, are you upset about what God is upset about? If so, you still face a challenge: how will you seek redemptive justice and avoid the temptation to exact destructive vengeance?

It's worth pausing here for a moment to point out that the majority of *bad* anger actually falls into this latter category; most destructive vengeance aims at some real (though usually exaggerated) injustice! You are in the greatest danger when you are *right*, because being right about someone else's sin so easily blinds you to your own. Nothing makes it harder to take the log out of your own eye than being able to say, "But she shouldn't have done that; it was wrong!"

This means that you must be exceedingly careful not to rush straight from evaluating something around you as wrong to unsheathing your sword. Instead, when your anger does indeed have a healthy seed, you must also evaluate if the responses your anger is urging are healthy as well. You must probe your own heart for pettiness, vindictiveness, self-righteousness, and the like, which want to stow away underneath your evaluation that the other person is in the wrong.

In short, evaluate *all* the facets of your anger. Don't stop digging just because you've unearthed one genuine injustice. Just as one fossilized bone likely indicates the rest of the skeleton is nearby, expect to find bad things in your own heart when your search turns up wrongdoing in others.

At other times, however, your anger will not flow from an even partially valid moral judgment. As sinners, we all hate things God does not hate. Our selfishness, self-pity, and arrogance all naturally target friends and blessings instead of enemies or curses. While this is the simplest kind of anger to respond to (repentance is always the next step), it is painfully hard to admit to yourself that your anger is plain old wrong. And, even when you do admit it, you are now butting up against some significant disordered love in your heart, and that means letting go of your anger will be a difficult process indeed. We'll say more about responding to sinful anger in the next section.

Then, on top of the times when our anger brazenly comes from sinful motives, we also face the challenge of communication between limited human beings in a confusing and complex world. As a result, our anger often rises against things we misunderstand. Friendly banter gets taken seriously: "I thought you meant next week, but you actually meant this week. Your idea of how much depth was needed in order to say 'we talked about it' and mine are different." Evaluating your anger can spare you a lot of heartache if you take the time to ask yourself questions like *Am I sure that is what they meant?* or *Does this line up with how this person tends to treat me and others in general?* If you have any doubt at all, slow down and follow up in the hope that you've misunderstood, wrestling to keep your anger at bay until you are sure!

Righteous anger—anger that aligns with God's—is most common when the object of the anger is someone else, not yourself. Jesus, for example, is agonized but not angry when he himself is nailed to the cross. However, he is incensed when flipping over the tables of money changers in the temple who are exploiting his brothers and sisters ("den of robbers" he calls them—Matt. 21:13) and insulting his heavenly Father ("Do not make my Father's house a house of trade"—John 2:16).

This doesn't mean anger at sin against oneself is wrong! God's anger, both in the Old and the New Testaments, is aroused when his people betray him. The examples in Scripture, however, are weighted heavily toward righteous anger that focuses on the injustices *others* face.

Finally, then, Scripture sees both good and bad in anger. The Bible's emphasis regarding human anger, however, is on its dangers and the ease with which it drives us to add to the carnage rather than to the constructive work of justice and restoration. James 1:20 sums up the danger well, saying that "the anger of man does not produce the righteousness of God." Every last one of us knows this from experience. Can anger be good and constructive? Ephesians 4:26 plainly shows that it can. The normal outcome of human anger, however, is destruction and chaos, which is why James warns so strongly against this emotion that so easily unleashes the tongue (and worse), and why we need to evaluate it rigorously in ourselves.

Acting in Response to Anger

As a rule, anger is dangerous. Here is the slightly more detailed rule of thumb: anger that you act on instinctively, without thinking it through, is so likely to be sinful and godless that you might as well say "always." If you want to live out of righteous anger, you need to start by slowing down.

We'll say it again: when you're angry, slow down.

You will almost never go wrong by pausing before you act when you are angry. Anger in the raw, like radioactive uranium, is deadly unless harnessed with exquisite caution. If you bring it out into the open without careful preparation, you will poison everything within a ten-mile radius. If we turn back to the first chapter of James again, we find James making this same point right next to the verse about man's anger not leading anywhere good. "Be quick to hear, slow to speak, slow to anger," he urges (James 1:19). Or, as pastor and author Zack Eswine put it, we need to "wait out [our] racing thoughts and emotions until [we] can choose good, even for an enemy."[3]

Thankfully, there are a lot of ways to slow down. Count to ten in your head before you respond. Take a deep breath. Talk about the matter later, after you've cooled down. In short, slowing down means taking time to think before you act when angry.

---

3. Zack Eswine, *The Imperfect Pastor: Discovering Joy in Our Limitations through a Daily Apprenticeship with Jesus* (Wheaton, IL: Crossway, 2015), 125.

Another really basic yet surprisingly helpful response to anger is to simply acknowledge that you are angry. I (Alasdair) was so proud of my six-year-old daughter this week, who, in the midst of several simultaneous disappointments, did not follow her normal pattern of screaming or kicking the middle seat in our van, but instead calmly said, "Dad, I'm so mad I could just tear this whole car up." To name anger rather than spray it at everyone around you is a great step of maturity and tends to help you respond *to* your anger rather than respond *in* your anger.

Doing this well is really hard, but really important. Anger is dangerous enough when shared and processed and brought well to the Lord. It is lethal in isolation. This doesn't mean you go to the person you are angry with and say, "Here's why I'm so furious with you." It does mean that if you see anger in your heart, you want to bring someone else in. We all need help bringing our anger to the Lord and thinking about constructive responses to wrongdoing, rather than ranting or gossiping about what others have done.

Make no mistake: action—albeit a carefully controlled and constructive action—is the right and good goal of anger! Righteousness does *not* mean doing nothing. Once you've taken your own heart to the Lord and to your brothers and sisters as best you can, you are called to act with redemptive, merciful boldness. With the log in your own eye gone—or at least chopped up—you will have the chance to help the person next to you with the ugly speck in his or her eye. Remember, God's anger is fiercer than yours or mine ever could be, yet look what he does with it. He disciplines his people *in order to bring us back*. He rebukes *in order to convict our hearts and turn us to repent*. Our God ultimately poured out his wrath on Christ, unleashing his fury without restraint one time and one time only, *so that those with whom he is angry might be restored*. True love attacks evil with vigor, and yet the attack is always a rescue mission. Our God is never bitter, petty, or cruel. Instead, his anger is always part of his larger purpose:

protecting and upholding all that he loves (and every sinner who begs his forgiveness becomes the treasure of his heart) to the praise of his glory.

Anger's Antidote

Ultimately, the best thing you can do about anger in your life is to cultivate humility. Humility empowers the healthy anger that treats others as more important than yourself. Humility protects others while exposing and undercutting the unhealthy anger that enthrones you as judge from a moral high ground only you perceive.

What are the earmarks of humility in the face of anger? Humility speaks honestly about what it knows and what it doesn't. You'll often hear humility say things like "It seems to me . . ." and "My concern is . . ." rather than "You always . . ." or "I can't believe you would. . . ." It asks real questions, and listens to the answers, whereas self-righteous anger seizes the microphone and rants. Humility assumes that others might have good reasons for doing things that have bothered us. Even when the fault lies entirely on the other side, humility recognizes the log in one's own eye and extends grace to offenders (which doesn't mean erasing all consequences), because it knows that Jesus has shown us grace beyond compare.

Questions for Reflection

As you deal with your own anger:

1. Where do you get frustrated, irritated, or annoyed? Does it bother you to think of those as instances of your being angry?
2. What is your go-to response to feeling angry? Do you avoid the situation? Placate others? Scheme revenge but smile in the meantime? Yell and make a scene? Numb yourself?
3. When have you felt angry recently? Have you brought it to God and others? What would it look like to act constructively in your anger? Will you?

As you help others with anger:

1. Galatians 6:1–2 points out that trying to help others when they are caught in sin tempts you to sin as well. What is your most common temptation when you engage with angry people? To become angry in return? To withdraw? To buy into their way of thinking?

2. Do you get angry in right ways on behalf of others? If so, do you tend to act constructively when you do?

15

Engaging Grief

Most of us have lost someone or something important to us. If you have, you're familiar with grief. The larger the loss, the greater the ache, and the deeper the sadness. If you've experienced the end of an intimate relationship or the death of a dear loved one, then you know the sadness can be so profound that it is difficult to describe.

You've probably also realized that there is more to grief than sadness. Of course, sadness often plays a starring role, but grief involves more than sadness or any other particular emotion. When you're grieving, you may feel many different emotions, some of which may surprise you—like anxiety, anger, or even relief. C. S. Lewis was surprised by what he called "the laziness of grief" after the death of his wife. He wrote, "I loathe the slightest effort."[1] Grief is a complex experience that we must engage carefully.

What Is Grief?

What Grief Communicates

Let's begin by thinking of grief broadly as the experience of loss. *Grief* is the umbrella word over the vast mix of things you feel

---

1. C. S. Lewis, *A Grief Observed* (New York: HarperOne, 1961), 5. Lewis continues: "Only as a dog-tired man wants an extra blanket on a cold night; he'd rather lie there shivering than get up and find one. It's easy to see why the lonely become untidy; finally, dirty and disgusting."

when you lose something or someone important to you. Grief communicates, "I've lost something important to me and I need you." (The "need you" part is the person or thing you lost and the others whose help you need in order to recover. We'll explore this more in a moment.)

Think of the word *grief* as a kind of picture frame that fits around all of the different things you might feel when you experience loss. For instance, you've probably heard about different "stages" of grief—denial, anger, bargaining, depression, and acceptance—based on Elisabeth Kübler-Ross's well-known theory of bereavement.[2] But try not to think about grief as a series of fixed steps. Instead, think of these five emotions and the many others you are experiencing as the swirling paints on a collage framed and entitled "Grief."

Grief over any good thing, including any good relationship, points us Godward. Grief hurts deeply because we are so aware of just how good a gift God had given us in that close friend, the physical ability to go for a walk, the chance to live near family, or the souvenir your dad brought back from abroad and gave you when you were ten years old. The anguish we feel when we lose things we love implicitly declares God's goodness in having given them. Our grief, then, can become the cry "Maranatha," come Lord Jesus, and make this broken world whole.

How Grief Relates

Understanding grief as the experience of loss can help us to understand how God intends it to work in our relationships, especially if we've lost a loved one. Though God's work in the midst of our grief often includes times when we need to process our grief alone, in general, we seek the presence and comfort of others. When our losses remind us of the unique connection to the person or thing

---

2. Elisabeth Kübler-Ross, *On Death and Dying: What the Dying Have to Teach Doctors, Nurses, Clergy and Their Own Families* (New York: Scribner, 1969, 2014); Elisabeth Kübler-Ross and David Kessler, *On Grief and Grieving: Finding the Meaning of Grief through the Five Stages of Loss* (New York: Scribner, 2014).

we loved, we can feel isolated and alone. As a result, we rightly yearn for the simple presence of others who represent relationship and love that *hasn't* been lost, and the hope of recovery. We may experience an emotional longing for others in a way we normally don't. And yet the diverse experiences of grief can make connecting with others more difficult than we might expect. Understanding the diversity of grief can help us give each other permission to experience and process grief differently.

I (Alasdair) remember one of the first men I ever counseled, who had lost his father to cancer shortly after my own dad had died from cancer. We were the same age, had similar upbringings, were both oldest brothers, and both had faith in Christ at the center of our lives. But I quickly realized that his struggles were completely different from mine. I am very thankful that just as I was getting my start in counseling, I learned that two people grieving the same event at the same time may do so in very different ways. Here are two more examples.

Parents grieving a child. I (Winston) once counseled a couple whose young-adult child died in an accident. The couple were happily married and loved each other very much, but they were struggling with feeling out of sync with each other's grief.

At one point, one parent was angry: "I can't believe he did this to us. Why wasn't he more careful?!" But the other parent was surprised by this and responded: "Why are you angry with him? I would do anything just to smell his hair one more time!" Both loved their son very deeply and were in agony, but each was experiencing it in a distinct way at that particular time. As we continued counseling, the roles sometimes reversed; the angry parent was sad and the sad parent was angry. At yet other times one parent was having a moment of relief while the other was despairing. To their credit, they learned to see the other's grief, no matter how different, as valid and even complimentary to their own.

A church grieving a pastor. At the church where I (Winston) serve as pastor, the previous pastor died very tragically and unexpectedly just three months before I arrived. Like the pastor of any church, he had different kinds of relationships with different members. Some were very close to him. One person told me that he hadn't lost just his pastor but also his best friend. Another, wanting to make sure my feelings weren't hurt, explained to me, "Sometimes I have to step out of the service on Sundays because it's just too painful to see you up there doing the things he's supposed to be doing." I totally understood and was not offended. For many, my presence was a painful reminder that something very wrong had happened. It wasn't personal; it was just grief.

Others had lost a spiritual mentor—someone they trusted to teach truth, dispense wisdom, baptize their children, and visit them when they were sick. Their grief was deep too, but in a different way. They were shocked and saddened, but their grief was moderated by the fact that a new spiritual leader had arrived. My presence wasn't as painful for them, even though they had lost a dear friend.

Still others were saddened to have lost their pastor but didn't have as intimate a relationship as the first two groups. They were thankful for and missed their pastor, but after several months they were ready to put the pain behind them and no longer felt the need to process it publicly.

A few months after I arrived, I offered an adult elective on grief. The participants were mostly the first group, those most intimately connected to the late pastor, and a few from the second group. They understandably felt the need to gather and share in their grief together. For them, grief was going to be a long journey, and they needed each other on that journey. Others weren't grieving at that level and didn't need that kind of support. I was careful to explain to the congregation that the class was for people who felt they needed it and that attendance was not a measure of whether or not they cared or were grieving. No group was more

holy or righteous than any other. Each group had a different relationship with the pastor and needed a different kind of support.

It's pretty basic, but it's a critical foundation for relating in
the midst of grief: grief can feel all kinds of ways. Understanding
and accepting this is vital in helping us move toward one another
during seasons of grief.

How Grief Motivates

If we think of grief as the experience of loss, then we can begin
to understand how it motivates us to seek comfort in connection
and care from others. Beneath the varied emotional experiences of
grief is a signal to God and others that says, "I am hurt and I need
you." And yet, sometimes, we may try to hide the fact that we are
grieving, out of embarrassment or not wanting to burden others.
Maybe we feel like we've been grieving too long, or we're afraid
others are getting tired of our grief. But when we do this, we keep
ourselves from receiving the care we legitimately need and risk having our emotions misunderstood. If you are feeling this way, try to
notice that most people intuitively respond to grief with care. Grief
is like a wound, and our instinct to be compassionate and caring
is a basic reflex of love. In the same way that we pick up the slack
for someone with a physical injury, bringing food or taking care of
other tasks the person is unable to perform, we may also need to
do relational and emotional work on behalf of the one who grieves.

For example, imagine you encounter a friend who is very angry,
and, hoping to be helpful, you ask, "What's bothering you? Why
are you so *angry*?" If in response your friend snaps, "Mind your
own business!" you might feel defensive or angry yourself. But
if, instead, your friend says, "My sister just died," you probably
soften immediately and respond, "Oh . . . that's terrible. I understand . . . I'm so sorry." Once you realize someone is grieving,
you take a different emotional stance and respond with care
and concern. Without even thinking about it, you are operating
within a grief framework.

Or imagine you encounter a colleague or coworker who is unusually distracted and withdrawn, and you ask, "Are you okay? You seem distracted and distant today." If the person responds, "I'm not doing well. My mother died yesterday," you don't say, "Well, we've got a job to do, so snap out of it and focus!" That would be monstrous. Instead you probably say something like, "Oh no! I'm so sorry to hear that. Why don't you take the rest of the day off and go home? I'm sure everyone will understand."

If the bereaved in these examples didn't share that they were grieving, or you didn't realize anger or distraction are normal experiences of grief, you might not know how to respond. Learning to speak our grief can help others respond to our grief with compassion and care rather than confusion and frustration.

How Should We Engage Grief?

Every loss is a broken connection. If you think of your life as a meaningful web of connected people, things, and events, then grief is what you experience when one of those strands is ripped out of the web. It doesn't just leave a hole where it once was; the threads that connected it to other things are left dangling, and the things that were supported by it are weakened as well. Whether you've lost a job, your health, your status, or a friend or family member, you've become untethered from something that anchored you and gave meaning to your day-to-day life. Engaging grief will mean reconnecting to everything the loss touches upon in a new way. You will have to reconsider and reacquaint yourself with everything that you associated with what has been lost by identifying, examining, and evaluating the loss in a way that connects you to God and others.

Identifying Grief

This is a simplistic analogy for grief, but we still think it rings true: Do you remember, when you were a little kid, how for a day or two after you lost a tooth, you kept sticking your tongue into the socket where to tooth once was? You just couldn't help it. There was this weird fascination with the hole where the tooth used to be. But eventually you were no longer fascinated by it. You had explored it, accepted the new situation, and moved on. Of course, there's nothing really tragic about losing a tooth in most cases, and the significant losses of our lives are more complicated. But, in a basic sort of way, that's how we engage grief. We identify and begin to absorb the loss by exploring and naming the contours of what was there, emotionally pressing into the grooves and holes left behind, and sharing the experience with others who love us well.

Over the last year my (Winston's) church started a bereavement support group of about ten to twelve people led by a parishioner with experience facilitating groups. Some were grieving the loss of a spouse, some a friend or family member, and some were there to understand how to support others who were grieving. Of course, part of our time was spent in prayer and thinking about what the Bible has to say about grief and loss, but much of our time was spent identifying and naming the losses by talking about and telling stories about those we missed: "Tell us who this person was and what he or she meant to you. What were the joys of the relationship? What do you miss the most?"

Group members brought in photographs and mementos to help us connect and care. We even wrote letters to those we'd lost and read them to the group. It was a powerful experience and very healing. It was a luxury for me to function more as a member of the group than a leader. I shared about the recent deaths of my own parents and all the ways I still wrestled with that. We even gathered as a group to watch a football game together at my house. It just seemed natural to connect with those who had shared with each other in such an intimate and healing way.

Reconnection and healing happen when we are able to identify the loss and share it with people who care. Because we are practicing the possibility of new life and reconnection after the loss, each person finds his or her unique way of revisiting the wound in order to facilitate healing.

Examining Grief

To get a bead on your grief, it's always helpful to examine it through the lens of Scripture. Because the Bible is about real life, the Bible tells the story of grief. From beginning to end, we witness terrible losses, the bereavement and groaning of God and his people, and the certain hope that renewed life follows these losses. Jump in anywhere you like and you will hear the vast range of emotions described in prose, proclaimed in poetry, and memorialized in song. You will also hear God acting and speaking in ways that point us to his promise to reverse the ravages of loss and death through Jesus.

We've always found David to be a good companion in grief. As you walk with him through his grief, you can get a sense of its many varieties and expressions. You may remember that David's life took a terrible turn when he caved into lust and essentially raped Bathsheba, then arranged for her husband's death on the battlefield. The results were disastrous. The prophet Nathan confronted David, telling him that the child conceived with Bathsheba would die and that his own wives would later be taken from him by someone close to him. Sure enough, the child died shortly after he was born. Years later the second part of Nathan's prophecy came to pass. Another of David's sons, Absalom, tried to steal the throne and publicly humiliate David by sleeping with his concubines in full public view. Though David tried to spare his life, Absalom was killed during the suppression of the rebellion.

David's experience illustrates the many forms of grief.

The grief of guilt. After being confronted by Nathan, David was stricken by guilt for his sin against God. In Psalm 51 David pours out his grief before God and pleads for forgiveness:

> Let me hear joy and gladness;
>   let the bones that you have broken rejoice.

Hide your face from my sins,
    and blot out all my iniquities. (vv. 8–9)

Grief may be an occasion for reflecting on our own failures or sin. Maybe, as in David's case, it's guilt over things we've done—our responsibility for a failed marriage, a lost job, or some other tragedy. Maybe it's guilt over squandered opportunities, things we wish we'd said or done but just never got around to. In any case, the Bible gives us words for speaking and sharing our guilt with God and others.

The grief of death. David also grieved the illness and impending death of his child. The Bible tells us that David pleaded with God. He fasted and "lay all night on the ground." He couldn't be persuaded to get up, and he wouldn't eat until after the child had died (2 Sam. 12:15–23). We expect to be struck with grief after the death of a loved one, but, as was the case with David, sometimes we can see death coming. Sometimes loved ones succumb to cancer or other degenerative disease, and we experience their death in agonizing slow motion. Later, after Absalom's death, David was grief-stricken again: "O my son Absalom, my son, my son Absalom! Would I had died instead of you, O Absalom, my son, my son!" (2 Sam. 18:33). Death will likely prove to be one of the most powerful experiences of grief you ever have. Expect to need a lot of help and companionship to find the words to express it.

The grief of betrayal. We don't know exactly what prompted David to pen Psalm 55, but it is rife with the agony and grief of personal betrayal. So it's possible that David wrote this as he wrestled with Absalom's treachery.

My heart is in anguish within me;
    the terrors of death have fallen upon me.
Fear and trembling come upon me,
    and horror overwhelms me. . . .

For it is not an enemy who taunts me—
    then I could bear it;

it is not an adversary who deals insolently with me—
    then I could hide from him.
But it is you, a man, my equal,
    my companion, my familiar friend.
We used to take sweet counsel together;
    within God's house we walked in the throng. (Ps. 55:4–5,
        12–14)

Betrayal comes in a million forms: a spouse commits adultery, a business partner embezzles money, close friends launch a campaign of gossip against you. You name it—betrayal can feel like your heart has been ripped out and stomped on. Though it may feel like too much for words, God has spoken the unspeakable and invites us to use his words as we pour out our hearts.

Grief of any kind. Psalm 31 is another of David's psalms. We aren't told the occasion for this one, which reminds us that the experience of grief is broad and not limited to just a handful of situations. David says:

Be gracious to me, O LORD, for I am in distress;
    my eye is wasted from grief;
    my soul and my body also.
For my life is spent with sorrow,
    and my years with sighing;
my strength fails because of my iniquity,
    and my bones waste away. (Ps. 31:9–10)

Grief can come to us in many shapes and forms, but when you examine it, don't feel pressured to categorize it. Sometimes grief can just be grief. Whatever losses you experience, you will find the Bible full of words to help you examine and express them.

Evaluating Grief

One of the hallmarks of being a Christian is the way we respond to grief. At one level our grief is unremarkable. We are as subject to the ups, downs, and entire range of emotional responses as everyone else. Yet our grief *is* different. Paul instructs the Thessalonians so that they will "not grieve as others do who have no hope" (1 Thess. 4:13). In Christ, no matter what we've lost, no matter how severe the grief, we have hope. If you find that for days on end there is no relief, no hint that things will ever get better, you may be grieving without hope and need help to connect with the hope you have in Christ.

In short, our hope is this: Jesus was raised from the dead and so conquered death. Think about the implications of that for your grief. It's more than the promise of life after death or your own resurrection. It actually means that Jesus has conquered *all losses* and will ultimately heal and restore them. Think of death as the ultimate loss that represents all other losses. Think of every smaller loss as a daily reminder that *everything* is moving toward dissolution, decay, and death. Death is the inevitable end for everything in a fallen world; it all perishes, spoils, and fades (see 1 Pet. 1:4) until it is gone and "its place knows it no more" (Ps. 103:16). We tend to avoid thinking about loss in those terms because doing so seems depressing. But unless we make the connection, we won't appreciate the scope of Jesus's salvation. Yes, Jesus's resurrection gives us hope so that we don't have to fear our own death, but we are meant to experience the power of his resurrection in the here and now as well.

In the first chapter of Paul's letter to the Ephesians he says that he prays that they may know "what is the immeasurable greatness of [God's] power toward us who believe," which is like the power that was at work in Christ when God "raised him from the dead" (Eph. 1:19–20). Paul then says that by grace, "even when we were dead in our trespasses," God "made us alive together with Christ" (Eph. 2:4–5). In other words, the power of God that raised Jesus from the dead is at work in us *now*. Resurrection power, the power to overcome death and all that it represents, isn't just for "later" but is for life in the here and now. It is the power to overcome all the losses of life in a fallen world.

Whenever we experience grief, whether through someone's death or a smaller loss, we need to remember that if we are united to Christ, loss never has the final word, and so we have hope. Our stories have been united to Jesus's story, so just as he overcame death and loss, so shall we. Grief is still a part of our lives, but we always have hope because the One who loves us has overcome death and loss and gives us his power and love even in the midst of grief. He gives us not just the words to speak and connect but also the power to do it and the love and reconnection that happen as we do.

Acting in Response to Grief

It's not wrong to want grieving people to feel better. It's a sign that you love them and wish they weren't in so much pain. It's understandable that grief seems like a problem that needs to be fixed, and it's difficult not to let the desire to provide care degenerate into "fixing." But a better approach is to view helping not as "making it better" but as being someone's companion in the journey through grief to healing.

Be a companion, not a fixer.

Speak to the isolation and the shame that often come with grief. It's important to remember that people going through grief, especially over a tragedy, don't necessarily know how it's "supposed" to feel. And you don't want to tell grieving individuals that they should feel one way and not another. Care for the grieving by reminding them that they're allowed to feel one way one day and a different way the next day, or even ten minutes later. You might say, "You're probably feeling all kinds of things that you weren't expecting." And then be silent and let them respond to that. Sometimes there will be anger, sometimes fear, and at other times *even relief.*

For example, sometimes grief means that someone has lost a loved one with Alzheimer's who was bedridden for months and for whom the grieving person was providing care. She may feel

relieved and resentful on the very same day. You can help her engage her grief by giving her permission to feel all kinds of things,
and to feel them at different times. Practice sensitivity to the fact
that grief is just as much about a lost *connection* as it is about a
lost person or object. Spare those in grief the additional suffering
of isolation and shame from well-meaning friends.

Jesus Overcomes Grief

Remember that grief, the experience of loss, is sometimes more
than sadness and may involve almost any emotion. Engaging grief
wisely requires us to be flexible and make room for those varied
experiences, especially when different people are grieving the same
thing at the same time but in very different ways. Be compassionate and patient with the bereaved, help them connect with God
and others by inviting them to share their grief in their own time
and in their own way. And know that God "gets" our grief. Every
page of Scripture speaks to both the pain of grief and the hope we
have in Christ. But above all, remember that Jesus has overcome
every loss and gives us his power and love to find life even after
the most terrible losses.

Questions for Reflection

As you deal with your own grief:

1. Name and describe as many different emotions as you've expe-
    rienced in your grief.
2. Read through any of the psalms explored in this chapter, or
    find another that accurately captures how your grief feels. Once
    you've read it through and meditated on it, write it out in your
    own words, as if it were your own. Share this in prayer with God
    and a trusted friend or counselor.
3. Think of moments when you've felt hope. Put your hope into
    words, if you can, and share them with a friend. Consider your
    hope a gift from God, and explore how it reflects his love for you
    in Christ.

As you help others with grief:

1. Practice listening to others talk about their grief, and let your sole focus be on deeply understanding and emotionally responding to their loss. Do your best to understand what their experience is like for *them*, and share your understanding with them. Don't try to fix it! Let your patient care convey the love of Christ.

2. Locate a grieving person in your life. Whether the loss is of a loved one, a job, health, a home—someone you know is there! Pray for and then reach out to that person. Ask how you can support him or her, and then do it.

3. Consider yourself a grieving person. It's a given in some realm of your life. If you are uncomfortable with grief, take time to understand your own before trying to help others.

16

Engaging Guilt and Shame

A young man wakes up outside. His hunger kept him up late the night before. Unable to afford food, he hasn't eaten in days. The rotting fruit meant for animals he's been hired to feed looks strangely appetizing.

He thinks all day, every day, about his family. He misses them—especially his dad—but he can't go back. He hurt them too much. He's a "toxic" person, as his older brother told him when the young man left. How did he get here?

In the parable of the prodigal son, Jesus explains that this man has asked for his share of the inheritance from his father, spent it all on foolish indulgence, and, out of desperation, hired himself out as a farmhand in a foreign country.[1] Two things stand out about his condition:

- He is *guilty*: He has done something wrong and worthy of punishment: he has dishonored his father and broken the relationship. By asking for his inheritance in advance he has, in effect, wished his father dead.
- He is *ashamed*. He feels changed—so defiled that he can't imagine a way back home, at least as a son. The only thing

---

1. Luke 15:11–32.

overcoming his sense of shame is his will to survive. He
hopes he might be tolerated as a servant but is certain he'll
never again be accepted as a son.

What hope can there be for him? Surely his father will never take
him back. But in desperation, he decides to go back—to face the
shame and ask to be a servant of his family. But when his father
sees him from a long way off, his father runs to him and kisses him
before he ever says a word. The father is vulnerable and welcoming toward his son, even *throwing a party* to celebrate his return.
Why? Though we appreciate the story, we find it hard to believe
that a father would really do this without some kind of proof that
this wayward son was sincere and the father wasn't being fooled.

Guilt and shame both come into play. Guilt awakens the son
to his sin. He knows that he's done wrong. Shame tells him that
there's no hiding what he's done, but perhaps shame's most damaging effect is that he feels defiled and different now. Guilt leaves
open the possibility of a way back, a way to make things right.
Shame isn't always so optimistic. But the father's love promises
that there is *always* a way home.

Before we understand how God's love invites us to engage guilt
and shame, let's explore what they are.

What Are Guilt and Shame?

What Guilt and Shame Communicate

Guilt communicates, "I've done something wrong." Shame communicates, "Something is wrong with me and others can see it."[2]

Guilt and shame can be two dimensions of one event—I've
done something wrong *and* there are *witnesses*. Whether from the
same event or not, guilt suggests that I have sinned, while shame
suggests that there is something about me that, if seen by others,
would be unacceptable.

---

2. Edward T. Welch, *Shame Interrupted: How God Lifts the Pain of Worthlessness and Rejection* (Greensboro, NC: New Growth, 2012), 11.

As with fear, anger, and grief, guilt and shame can be very valuable when they are telling the truth. If I have sinned, both guilt and shame can help me to see that I have. To be called "shameless" is not a good thing. Also, if you have been mistreated and sinned against by others, shame rightly alerts you to the wrongness of their actions, just as a sharp pain in your abdomen alerts you to a rupturing appendix. When guilt and shame accurately identify problems, wrongs can be righted and relationships restored.

However, guilt and shame can be incredibly damaging if they become warped. When guilt is warped, it becomes self-condemnation, arguing that no forgiveness is possible. When shame is warped, it becomes self-loathing. If guilt and shame have become my identity, then I can't imagine ever removing the stain I feel without removing myself. I am so defiled that I am fundamentally damaged and less than everyone else. Such experiences of guilt and shame are more often the result not of what we've done but of what has been done to us.

How Guilt and Shame Relate

Both guilt and shame are meant to alert us to a break in our relationships. Both emotions are fundamentally about our connections with other people. Remember what we said earlier about how emotions connect us to others like the parts of the body. When you feel pain in a part of your body, it is telling you of a problem that needs attention. Without the pain, you might go on damaging your body without realizing it. In the same way, painful emotions such as guilt and shame are, at their best, meant to promote healing and growth. When we get a "signal" via guilt and shame, we know something's gone wrong. Time to examine our relationships.

Guilt communicates that we've failed to live up to a goal—that we've missed the mark. Biblically, our goals are always *relational*. Jesus has taught us that the whole of the law can be summarized in two commandments: *love God and love neighbor*

(Matt. 22:34–40; Mark 12:28–31). Guilt, reflected in a healthy conscience, provides guardrails to help us know when we're acting against God or neighbor. Guilt, in itself, doesn't tell us that we are fundamentally *unable* to love; it tells us when we've failed to do so. In that sense, guilt doesn't rob us of the hope that we can do better; it can have a positive role in our emotional lives.

Shame, too, reveals a break in relationship, but shame focuses more on how others see us and we see ourselves. Sadly, guilt and (in particular) shame can become reasons for isolation rather than reconciliation. When we choose to hide our guilt rather than engage it, shame tends to deepen our sense that we have something to hide. Once we start down the path of hiding, guilt and shame can begin to snowball, making it harder and harder to engage with them constructively and work toward restored relationships.

How Guilt and Shame Motivate

Guilt alerts a healthy conscience to wrongdoing and leads us to repentance. It is intended to motivate us to reconcile with God and neighbor. As noted above, even shame has a *limited* but important role in reconciliation. Shame typically comes to the foreground when guilt hasn't gotten the job done—say, when we've indulged our sin and been caught or fear being caught, perhaps when we are more committed to hiding the wrong than repairing it.

For example, if you've cheated on your spouse, you *should* feel guilty. You've broken your marital vow, betrayed your love, and likely harmed others as well—the one you've cheated with, that person's spouse, your children, and so on. You've failed to love God and neighbor.

But imagine that you are so blinded by sin that you resist the guilt meant to pull you away from that sin. And when found out, you still don't acknowledge how wrong you are. Consequences follow. Maybe you are asked to leave the home. Friends and neighbors find out. Perhaps your pastor is informed, and you are excluded from fellowship at church or asked to step down from responsibilities. *Now* you feel not only guilt but also shame. The community sees you differently. The guilt and shame *both* convince you to think more deeply about what you've done, and you finally repent.

This reflects the way Paul hopes guilt and shame will work in the Corinthian church. He urges the Corinthians to set an unrepentant man outside of the community: "You are to deliver this man to Satan for the destruction of the flesh, so that his spirit may be saved in the day of the Lord" (1 Cor. 5:5). Strong language—yet the hope and prayer are for reconciliation. The purpose is to prompt serious reflection and repentance in the guilty party. And it works. Once the man has repented, Paul urges the Corinthians to forgive and restore him to the community (2 Cor. 2:5–8). Sometimes we need guilt *and* shame to show us just how seriously we've sinned.

It's also critical to remember that, as noted above, guilt can be distorted and we may feel shame not because of what we've done but because of what others have done to us. In these instances guilt and shame can alert us to our need to confront those who have shifted blame onto us or otherwise wounded our consciences. Or when we've been shamed by others, shame can tell us that we've been wronged and urge us to seek the help and safety of others who can protect us and speak lovingly to our shame.

How Should We Engage Guilt and Shame?

Identifying Guilt and Shame

Like a lot of negative emotions, we can sometimes hide guilt and shame from ourselves. It's easier not to face them, so we pretend they don't exist. The good voices of guilt and shame—*I shouldn't have done that, and it has consequences*—can easily become *I hate myself, and I want to be invisible*. Sometimes it's hard to hear the good intentions of guilt and shame, so we try to shut them up by dulling our consciences with denial and escapism. We avoid people we would normally enjoy. We indulge in activities that produce more-pleasant feelings. But this road is a lie. Simply suppressing the voices in these emotions is the road to death.

Sometimes guilt and shame hide under the guise of anger and blame shifting. We see this from the very beginning of Scripture. In Genesis 3, Adam and Eve choose to hide after sinning against God by eating the forbidden fruit. When God calls them out, Adam points at Eve and exclaims, "The woman whom you gave to be with me, she gave me fruit of the tree, and I ate" (Gen. 3:12). It seems that one of the basic reflexes of sin is to deflect guilt and shame onto another.

If we aren't used to identifying guilt and shame, they can hide under many distractions and other emotional responses, but anytime you find yourself moving away from others and concealing what's going on inside of you, it's worth asking yourself if you've done something wrong or you fear that others see you that way.

Examining Guilt and Shame

Guilt has both objective and subjective realities. In other words, you can *be* guilty but not *feel* guilty. Conversely, you can *feel* guilty but not truly *be* guilty. It's important to distinguish between the guilt we feel because we really have done something wrong and the guilt we may feel for other reasons. Sometimes the difference is described as *true guilt* versus *false guilt*. True guilt is about an objective moral failing: we really have done something wrong; we've violated God's law. False guilt is the result of a *perceived* moral failing rooted in something other than or in addition to God's law, whether cultural norms, a family's values, or simply others' expectations of us. True guilt and false guilt feel the same but are rooted in different criteria.

For instance, a child whose parents are divorced may *feel* guilty because his mother becomes sad whenever he leaves to visit his father on weekends. He *feels* responsible for his mother's sadness—but he isn't. Or consider the guilt that comes from "people pleasing," in which our God-given instinct to help others gets twisted into guilt that plagues us every time someone is disappointed or upset with us. False guilt happens when we break a law that isn't God's. This can be tricky to navigate because, when cultural and relational codes don't reflect God's values, they may *need* to be broken, though others will ask us to feel guilty for doing so. For example, you may receive a lot of pushback for refusing—out of love—to rescue a substance-abusing family member from legal consequences.

When it comes to shame, it's more helpful to think of the difference between *shame* and *being shamed*. Shame is an appropriate response to the consequences of sin, though it can be distorted and exaggerated. But *being shamed* is being sinned against and feeling defiled. For example, naming and exposing abusive patterns in one's own family may result in the whistle-blower being shamed—even feeling ashamed of himself—even though he hasn't done anything wrong. Often children who have been abused direct anger toward themselves because they learn that it is not safe to outwardly critique the abuser in the family. This produces a destructive sense of shame as well, an understandable but undeserved sense of badness. This too is being shamed.

But God is looking for us. And when we come forward, we find grace. In general, guilt and shame at their best should move us *toward* God and others. God's grace and love given in Christ provide an alternative to self-loathing, blame shifting, and hiding of every kind. A very helpful diagnostic for guilt and shame is to continue asking, *Is this moving me away from God and others or toward them?*

Evaluating Guilt and Shame

Guilt and shame can be very messy. Does my guilt mean that I really have done something wrong? Do I have something to repent of, or have I simply adopted someone else's disappointment? Does my shame mean that I need to face what *I've* done or what was done *to me*, or *both*? Even worse, guilt and shame can feel like an indictment of *who I am*—like I'm damaged goods, defiled, worthless, like the prodigal son living in a pigpen.

To find our way through this fog, we need a light, a beacon of hope and courage to move forward. That light is the love of God and the grace given to us in Jesus. God's grace is much more than an offer to remove guilt; it is the power to restore our identity, to provide a way home to true intimacy and fellowship with God.

Acting in Response to Guilt and Shame

What do we need in response to guilt and shame?

More than forgiveness. Once my (Winston's) wife's car was sideswiped while parked on the street in front of her office. Thankfully, the responsible party left a note on the windshield apologizing profusely, offering to pay for the repair, and providing all of her contact information. After a few phone calls and a trip to the body shop, the car was repaired and a check from the offender came in the mail.

All was forgiven. My wife never actually met the other person and never had more than one phone conversation with her, and that was okay. Neither my wife nor the other person was looking for a new friend; the two just needed to solve a problem. Guilt was acknowledged, the damage repaired, and they went back to their separate lives.

But that's not how it works with God.

God doesn't just want to remove our guilt; he wants intimate relationship with us. He is not just trying to fix a dent in his reputation that we've caused. His purpose is deeper than that. He wants to heal our identity by identifying with us, by becoming one with us. Restoration with God means being restored to our status as his beloved children.

God's extravagant grace. Grace is unearned favor, freely given. While this is often easy for us to understand, it is hard to practice, in part because many of us haven't seen it modeled very well. For some, finding forgiveness and restoration has felt more like groveling and being placed on probation, if they ever find forgiveness at all. So we must look beyond the failed efforts of others and trust what God has revealed to us through his Son, Jesus Christ.

Start by meditating on some of Jesus's amazing teaching on forgiveness and grace. Notice how often he teaches extravagant, even downright risky, expressions of forgiveness and grace. Hang out longer where this chapter started, in Luke 15. There the Pharisees and teachers of the law mutter about Jesus mingling with the guilty and shamed. Jesus tells his critics that God is like the shepherd who leaves the ninety-nine sheep to find the one that has wandered away. And what does he do when he finds the stray? Is he angry and punishing? No, he puts it on his shoulders, carries it home, and asks his friends and neighbors to rejoice with him. "I have found my sheep that was lost," he exclaims (Luke 15:1–7).

Still in Luke 15, a woman has ten silver coins and loses one. What does she do? Figure that a 10 percent loss isn't so bad? No! She lights a lamp and sweeps and searches until she finds the lost coin, and when she finds it, she asks all her friends to celebrate with her. Jesus concludes, "Just so, I tell you, there is joy before the angels of God over one sinner who repents" (Luke 15:10).

This is the extravagant love that Jesus displayed on the cross. By insisting on love and forgiveness in the midst of extreme trial, he defeated Satan (whose name comes from the Hebrew *satan*, meaning "accuser"—Job 1–2; Zech. 3:1). Jesus was lifted up, love was unbowed, retribution and payback were condemned, and forgiveness was freely proclaimed. We are free to practice forgiveness and mercy instead of payback and groveling because of Christ's victory. On a mission of love from his Father, Jesus reclaimed us from the possession of the Accuser and made us his children. We are no longer defiled, less than what he created us to be. We are his.

A new identity. We've said that we need more than forgiveness: we need a new association, a new identity. God doesn't just forgive us—he makes us new. Through Christ we are "a new creation" at the very core of our being (2 Cor. 5:17). When we are overcome with guilt and shame, we need help remembering our identity as God's children. As a Christian, when I sin, I am acting against my identity. Sin is not at the center of who I am. In Christ each of us is a *child of God*! We need to know that we are more than forgiven. In Jesus we have a new association, a new identity. Jesus overcomes shame by saying, "You belong to me."

Not going it alone. With the hope of God graciously connecting us to himself, honoring us, forgiving us, restoring relationship with us, and claiming us utterly and eternally as his, there is one enormously important action step we can take as a response in faith: talk about your guilt and your shame with someone else you trust. Do not listen to the voice inside that tells you to hide. Confessing your guilt and sharing your shame with a brother or sister in Christ has enormous power to free and heal your heart. Both guilt and shame were meant to drive us to step more fully into the light, cling more closely to Christ, and associate ourselves in word, deed, and identity with the One who has embraced us. But just as both guilt and shame lead to growth when exposed to light, both guilt and shame tend to fester in the dark.

What if the person you tell handles it poorly and condemns or shames you all the more? This is an appropriate fear. Still, there are two very good reasons to find someone to speak to. First, in many cases the excruciating vulnerability of sharing our guilt and shame makes us tend to exaggerate how badly others may be handling our opening up. Second, and more important, ultimately the choice to share and make yourself vulnerable to another person is not based on a guarantee that exposing your guilt or shame will lead to healing or even understanding from that person. Instead, the choice must be grounded in a trust that God has made us to need other people and that, no matter how the other person receives our words, God will be faithful to work in us, even through the pain of being misunderstood or wronged. Put more simply, speaking about guilt and shame is an act of trust in God and accepting our God-designed need for other people; and anything done in faith and obedience will have benefit to your soul, no matter what others do in response.

There Is Always a Way Home

Guilt and shame sometimes tempt us to flee relationships, to cover up and hide. Like the prodigal son, we find ourselves living far away from the things we really love and wonder if there is a way home. In Christ, there is always a way home. The love and grace of Jesus give us the freedom and power to face guilt and shame, whether they result from wrongs we've committed or from how others have wronged us. God solves guilt and shame by transferring their burden to the work of Christ, who takes evil seriously, takes mercy just as seriously, and deals with them both in the context of the home he is building for us through love. "Christ is faithful over God's house as a son. And we are his house" (Heb. 3:6).

Questions for Reflection

As you deal with your own guilt and shame:

1. Read through Luke 15 in its entirety. Choose one of Jesus's parables on grief as a focus of prayer and meditation for a week. Consider yourself the lost sheep, the lost coin, or the prodigal son. Commit to sharing things you learn with one other person.

2. Can you think of ways your understanding of right and wrong have changed over time? Are there things you used to see as wrong and feel guilty about but no longer view the same way? What has changed? How does that relate to Jesus's summary of the law, to love God and neighbor?

3. Think about one thing you feel shame over though you are not overwhelmed by that shame. Share that experience in prayer with the Lord, asking for his cleansing and healing. If you are able, end

your prayer by saying, "Thank you for loving me and making me your beloved child."

As you help others with guilt and shame:

1. People who feel shame don't often say so. Instead they may simply avoid letting others know them. Without making any assumptions about them, notice a few people in your life who seem isolated or withdrawn. Simply make an effort to reach out to them and slowly build relationships.

2. As you hear people you know expressing strong emotions, especially fear or anger, consider that they may be experiencing shame. What might cause them to feel shame? Think of a few simple ways to let them know you identify with them, and they belong.

17

A Museum of Tears

We've spent a lot of time talking about negative emotions: sadness, anger, fear, and so on. We've done that because the dark end of the emotional spectrum gives us the most trouble. Most of the time most of us don't see the value of these negative emotions, so we squash or surrender to them rather than bringing them to the Lord and engaging them well.

But learning to value and engage our dark feelings isn't the end of the story. One day, our negative emotions will no longer be necessary. "I will rejoice in Jerusalem / and be glad in my people," the prophet Isaiah says of the day when God makes all things new.

> No more shall be heard in it the sound of weeping
>   and the cry of distress. (Isa. 65:19)

Why will tears and distress clear off the stage? *Because they will no longer be needed.*

Isaiah goes on to list reasons why God's final coming will make tears obsolete. Our beloved children will not be in danger (65:20). Everyone will live out a fullness of days (which we learn in the New Testament means eternal life, not just dying at a ripe old age!—65:20). There will be perfect blessing on our work and our leisure (65:21–22). Nothing will threaten our peace or happiness (65:21). Families will be together forever without rebellion, separation, or tragedy (65:23). God will be in immediate contact with us and never distant (65:24). Danger and death and pain and injury and evil will vanish forever (65:25).

In short, it is not that we will be incapable of tears in heaven. It is that heaven will be a place where there simply won't ever be a reason to shed tears of grief.

Does this mean the ultimate goal of our emotional life is to put all our negative emotions behind us?

Not exactly.

The idea that, in heaven, we'll forget all the bad things done to us (or by us) is plausible and comforting on one level. But, while there are some verses (e.g., Isa. 65:17) that seem to suggest that forgetting our earthly suffering is precisely what will happen, the weight of Scripture is on the other side. We will indeed remember our lives and our trials here on earth.

And it will be beautiful to us.

How is this possible? The reason we will be able to remember our pain without reexperiencing it or having it poison our heavenly joy is that God himself has chosen not to forget or erase the reality of pain but, rather, to take it into his own heart. He will indeed wipe away every tear when he returns (Rev. 21:4), but, at the same time, he promises to keep your tears in a bottle because of his love and compassion for you (Ps. 56:8). Somehow heaven will be a place where our sorrows are both utterly and completely comforted and deeply and eternally remembered.

We named this chapter "A Museum of Tears" with this exact tension in mind. The end of the story really is radical, complete comfort. No more tears. Every earthly pain a "light momentary affliction" compared with the glory of heaven (2 Cor. 4:17). And yet the trials we've been through and the sins we've committed are exactly the things that now make our souls hunger and thirst for redemption and God's restoring all things. Our tears whet our appetite for heaven.

Ultimately, however, *our* tears pale in comparison with God's. The truly jaw-dropping thing is this: Jesus's pain in his time on earth changed him. Forever. The Bible tells us that Christ will be *eternally* the Lamb who was slain. The scars from the nails that pinned him to that cross are on his wrists right now, at this moment, as you read these words. And they always will be.

Do you grasp that our God took not just flesh but scars forever? How can we but worship at such love?

Let us be clear. This is not saying that God is suffering in heaven or that he has somehow lessened himself and marred his glory or even his joy. The exact opposite is true! His scars are the very emblems of his deepest, most shocking, most breathtaking goodness. His scars are *intrinsic to his glory*.

That means your scars and tears from the pain of life while trusting and waiting for his redemption will be glorious too.

Thus, although our sufferings will be more assuaged than we can now imagine, this won't be by pushing them to the side or ignoring them. Instead, we will worship with a joy of which the greatest thrills now are but a fleeting glimpse precisely *because* our sorrows, fears, wretchedly guilty failures, and shames have been so wonderfully redeemed. In fact, to be "the redeemed" is by definition to be those who know loss and pain in a way that drives love and adulation for our Savior who delivered us.

Somehow, heaven will be utterly without sadness and yet full of old sorrows so comforted that we may well weep with the poignancy of the joy. Somehow the kingdom come will be so whole that even the greatest brokenness we now find in our bodies and souls will become a source of praise. Somehow the guilt of fully seeing the destructive impact of our sin will lead to the ecstasy and relief of forgiveness.

Somehow, in some way, the depths of which we will never sound in this life, *every* emotion will one day resolve into joy.

In the meantime, we are right to delight in the comforts and blessings and joys and laughter God grants us. Yet we are also right to collapse on the ground and sob inconsolably, to bear on our hearts the weight of the dangers of those we love, and to set flinty eyes and clenched teeth against the evils that beset us. Now we sometimes laugh so hard we cry. Then all our crying will give way to laughter.

Meanwhile, we are also right to wait. We wait on a God who has chosen to have emotions toward us because that is an inescapable result of his choice to love us. And love us he has. A God who has first loved us is a God we can love. A God who has chosen to be moved is a God we can trust when we are moved. A God who has chosen to bear scars is a God we can trust with our wounds, knowing that all joys now are a mere foretaste, and all tears now are a precious prelude to complete comfort.

There is a time to laugh and a time to weep, but even those who weep can rest, remembering that blessed are those who mourn, for they shall be comforted. Every tear will be wiped away, each one ending its days as a treasure in the house of him whose smile will invite us to share his joy forever.

Appendix

Does God Really Feel?

The Doctrine of Impassibility

Does God Have Emotions?

Yes, God does have emotions.

Unpacking that truth, however, can be tricky. The discussion touches on an important point of theology: God's impassibility. If you are familiar with that doctrine, you know the theology can get technical and hard to follow pretty quickly. And, complicating matters, theologians don't all agree. For those of you new to the subject, impassibility is the doctrine that God is not able to suffer or be changed by involuntary passions.

The basic concern here is an important one: the Bible is clear that God is not dependent on his creation in any way (i.e., he is truly transcendent), and therefore he cannot be at its mercy, involuntarily affected by it, reeling in reaction to what he has made, and thus on some level controlled by it. In other words, what he has created cannot afflict him with suffering or *make* him feel anything.

Right off the bat you might think that it actually sounds like God *doesn't* have emotions. If God is unaffected by his creation, then—well—he can't *feel* anything about it good or bad. But that isn't what the doctrine of impassibility is getting at. The issue isn't really whether or not God *has* emotions but what they are like. Does God experience emotions the way we do? Some theologians argue that he *does* and that this is basic to his ability to empathize with us. Other theologians argue that he *does not* experience emotions as we do at all. If he did, his emotions would make him as willy-nilly as we are, and we could no longer consider him reliably stable (i.e., immutable).

Does It Really Matter?

This can sound a bit abstract and philosophical already, and you might be wondering, does impassibility really matter? It does. It really matters both that God has emotions and that they are different from ours in important ways.

God Really Understands and Cares for Us

For most of us it matters a great deal that God has emotions for very personal reasons. At stake is whether or not God really understands and cares about our experiences, especially our suffering. To say that God is impassible seems to suggest that perhaps he doesn't. Since he can't suffer, how could he possibly understand? And if he doesn't understand, how could he care? We want to know that God relates to us emotionally without having the problems that our emotions create for us.

So let us be clear: God *does* understand, and he *does* care.

Hopefully we've made it clear all along that Jesus provides the clearest understanding of both our emotions and God's. In particular, Jesus's role as High Priest demonstrates God's commitment to relating with us emotionally. We've referenced Hebrews 4 several times, but it's worth revisiting:

> For we do not have a high priest who is unable to sympathize
> with our weaknesses, but one who in every respect has been

tempted as we are, yet was without sin. Let us then with confidence draw near to the throne of grace, that we may receive mercy and find grace to help in time of need. (Heb. 4:15–16)

God's empathy is rooted in Christ's work. Jesus is our foundation for understanding how God relates to us emotionally.

God cared enough about understanding us that God the Son *stepped into our shoes* by taking on a human nature. Jesus's flesh and bone are proof that God has established a deep connection to our emotional experience and he wants us to know about it. In fact, he demonstrates his solidarity with us, in particular, through Jesus's *suffering*. Jesus's trials and temptations validate the bond he has with us as our Priest, the One who can truly represent us to God in our misery. Jesus really suffered as a flesh-and-blood human being. He really gets it, so when he tells us that he cares, we can know that he means it. And because he really gets it and experienced suffering without sin, God the Son can faithfully communicate that experience to his Father.

God's Emotions Are Different

But impassibility matters for other reasons as well. Some important attributes of God are at stake. In particular, whatever similarity exists between God's emotions and ours ought not undermine God's unchanging character (immutability), which undergirds his faithfulness and ability to save us.

So in what sense *does* God have emotions? Traditionally theologians have made a distinction between passions and affections. Historically *passions* described the more physical aspect of emotions, which, as we explained earlier, means that to some extent our bodies are always shaping our emotions. We don't want to say that about God, though, because God doesn't have a body, and God doesn't get cranky when his blood sugar drops. The church fathers used the term *passions* to describe what God *doesn't have* in order to defend against heresies which taught that the Father suffered on the cross[1] or that God compromised his divine nature[2] in order to accomplish salvation. In this sense, we ought to *deny* that God has passions. He is impassible, meaning that the creation or his creatures cannot push him around emotionally.

At the same time, this does not mean that God lacks *affections*, which we today might call "feelings." Traditionally, the word *affections* has described an emotion rooted in a moral value. Pastor and theologian Kevin DeYoung explains:

> If we are equating emotions with the old sense of passions, then God doesn't have emotions. But if we are talking about affections, he does. God's emotions are cognitive affections involving his construal of a situation. Most of what we call emotion in God is his evaluation of what is happening with his creation.[3]

DeYoung goes on to capture the core beauty of God's impassibility by saying that God "is love to the maximum at every moment. He cannot change because he cannot possibly be any more loving, or any more just, or any more good. God cares for us, but it is not a care subject to spasms or fluctuations of intensity."[4] Thus, while it might appear at first that the doctrine of God's impassibility will leave us with a cold, distant, and disconnected deity, instead the exact opposite is true: the glorious fact that God cannot and does not change means we can completely rely on his heart bursting with love, compassion, pity, tenderness, and anger at injustice; we can delight in his works, knowing he will always do them with

---

1. Patripassianism is an error of modalism, the belief that the Father, the Son, and the Holy Spirit are simply three "modes" of one being, rather than distinct persons; and so God the Father actually suffered on the cross.

2. Monophysitism is the heresy that Christ has only one nature instead of two, human and divine. Monophysitism would imply that Jesus suffered in his divine nature, making the divine contingent on the creation.

3. Kevin DeYoung, "'Tis Mystery All, the Immortal Dies: Why the Gospel of Christ's Suffering Is More Glorious because God Does Not Suffer" (edited transcript of a presentation at the T4G conference of 2010), 11, https://www.google.com/search?ei=1fl5W8jTNdGO5wL FiqLwBg&q=T4G-2010-KDY-v_2.pdf. DeYoung provides a more technical but very accessible discussion of impassibility.

4. DeYoung, "'Tis Mystery All," 9.

these attributes without tiring. God's impassibility is actually the grounding hope of our ability to know and trust his emotions.

Isaiah 49:15 says:

> Can a woman forget her nursing child,
> that she should have no compassion on the son of her
> womb?
> Even these may forget,
> yet I will not forget you.

Rob Lister applies this passage to God's emotional life:

> When we argue that God is impassible in the sense of being insusceptible to involuntary emotional manipulation, we mean that he is impassible not because he is affectively weak, but rather because he is affectively strong and full. God is more passionate than we are about the things that matter most.[5]

In other words, God doesn't have passions in that he is not jerked around by creation. God doesn't have "good" days and "bad" days. The early fathers were not arguing that God is *dispassionate* but rather speaking in a philosophically credible way about how God is *different* from creatures. But these impassibility formulations should not compel us to say that God is in no way like us emotionally. We are *passible* and God is *impassible*. God is *not* like us in some important ways, and he is *like* us in important ways. God is energetically enthused and emotionally invested in creation by his own free and consistent choice, but God's emotional life does not compromise his character or change his essence.

The Mystery of Faith

All Christian doctrine is at some point an expression of mystery. God is not just a different version of us; he is *distinct from us* as

---

5. Rob Lister, *God Is Impassible and Impassioned: Toward a Theology of Divine Emotion* (Wheaton, IL: Crossway, 2013), 215.

the Creator. Whether you're talking about the doctrine of the Trinity, the incarnation, or the problem of evil, everything is going to have a mystery at its bedrock. The goal of this appendix is not to say everything that can be said, but merely to point out that in order for us to know God *as God*, we must admit that we are knowing someone who transcends our complete understanding. While we affirm that what *can* be said about God can be said truly and accurately in so far as God has revealed himself to us, we must draw the line of mystery where God stops speaking.[6]

A Simple and Certain Hope

Let's return to the issue at stake for most readers of this book: When you're suffering, does God care? Of course God cares if you're suffering. Not only does he care; *he cares that you know he understands*. Because Jesus is our High Priest, Jesus in his human nature understands suffering existentially and physically. Because of both Jesus's purity and his human passion, God is uniquely qualified to empathize with you in Christ.

In order to keep a balanced view of God's emotional life, always return to the Trinity as the picture of the divine emotional life. The Father sympathizes with you and sends Christ to take an active role in your life. The Son empathizes with you directly through his human nature. And the Holy Spirit empathizes imminently through his indwelling in you (Rom. 8:26).

---

6. Incomprehensibility is the doctrine that God cannot be known exhaustively (see, e.g., Deut. 29:29).

General Index

Scripture Index

NOTES

Also Available from CCEF

For more information, visit **crossway.org**.

Restoring Christ to Counseling and Counseling to the Church

COUNSELING
ccef.org/counseling

WRITING
ccef.org/resources

TEACHING
ccef.org/courses

EVENTS
ccef.org/events

"CCEF is all about giving hope and help with a 'heart.' If you want to learn how to effectively use God's Word in counseling, this is your resource!"

Joni Eareckson Tada, Founder and CEO, Joni and Friends International Disability Center

"The vision of the centrality of God, the sufficiency of Scripture, and the necessity of sweet spiritual communion with the crucified and living Christ—these impulses that lie behind the CCEF ministries make it easy to commend them to everyone who loves the Church."

John Piper, Founder, desiringGod.org; Chancellor, Bethlehem College & Seminary

Christian Counseling & Educational Foundation
ccef.org